"Jeremy Kingsley's book encourages people to get up in faith and move on, giving practical steps for how to do that. It is a good read for anyone who has been knocked down by their own sin, by the opposition of the world, or by circumstances. I recommend it both because I know Jeremy and because I believe in his story."

Dick Lincoln
Pastor, Shandon Baptist Church
Columbia, South Carolina

"I have known Jeremy Kingsley for pretty much all of his life. I always knew he would be a great leader and influencer of people. He writes from personal experience as well as from his own close relationship with God. You will be encouraged and strengthened by reading this book. Your struggles will ⌐ ∽ spiritual perspective that is essential to be an overcomer in t⌐

Jerry Bruette
ıving Hope Church
ʀeen Bay, Wisconsin

"Practical. Genuine. Relevant. Auṫⁱᶜᵉⁿᵗ stor should encourage every person in their church to read *Getting Back Up*. It is filled with relevant truths all of us need to hear and apply to our lives."

Beau Eckert
Pastor, Calvary Church
Lancaster, Pennsylvania

"What do you do when everything you've planned falls apart? Jeremy offers much needed perspective and encouragement to those of us attempting to live significantly for Christ in the midst of great difficulty. Read this book. You'll laugh, cry, and be inspired!"

Mat Balgaard
Executive Pastor, Church of Celebration
Phoenix, Arizona

"Life is difficult but God is good. If hard times have already greeted your steps in life, take courage and enjoy how God might use this book to help you rise above the situation."

Greg P. Despres
Missional Life Pastor, Cypress Bible Church
Houston, Texas

"Jeremy Kingsley is one of the best communicators I know. He now extends his gifts to the written page. His life is rooted in God's Word and full of passion. You must hear him speak and you will be blessed by his book!"

Efrem Smith
Superintendent, Pacific SW Conference,
the Evangelical Covenant Church
Author, *The Hip Hop Church* and
Jump: Into a Life of Further and Higher

"I can say Jeremy Kingsley's ministry has had a transformational impact both in the ministries I've served in and in my own life over the last fifteen years. You will see in *Getting Back Up* his compelling way of communicating truth that inspires and challenges believers to want more of God in his or her life."

Todd Milby
Pastor, Summit Church
Estero, Florida

"As a person who knows first hand about the most intimate inner struggles and the challenging setbacks of life I know that *Getting Back Up* will serve as a companion and inspiration to overcome these trying times. Through simple strategies and inspirational stories, *Getting Back Up* will provide comfort, incite new hope, and instruct you as to how to fulfill the special purposes God has created you for."

William Prescott
Professional Strength and Conditioning Coach,
author of *Hope for Everyday*

"Jeremy has a knack for getting to the root of our problems when we are hit by circumstances that seem overpowering. As a trauma survivor, I found practical and fresh insights into moving on after things go bad. He points readers toward God and the bright future we all desire."

Craig DeMartino
After the Fall Ministry

GETTING BACK UP
WHEN LIFE
KNOCKS YOU DOWN

GETTING BACK
UP WHEN LIFE
KNOCKS YOU DOWN

JEREMY KINGSLEY

BETHANY HOUSE PUBLISHERS

a division of Baker Publishing Group
Minneapolis, Minnesota

Published by Bethany House Publishers
11400 Hampshire Avenue South
Bloomington, Minnesota 55438
www.bethanyhouse.com

Bethany House Publishers is a division of
Baker Publishing Group, Grand Rapids, Michigan

Printed in the United States of America

Library of Congress Cataloging-in-Publication Data
Kingsley, Jeremy.
    Getting back up when life knocks you down / Jeremy Kingsley.
        p.   cm.
    "A practical and inspiring guide for those recovering from difficult times"—Provided by publisher.
    Includes bibliographical references (p.   ).
    ISBN 978-0-7642-0908-6 (pbk. : alk. paper))
    1. Conduct of life—Religious aspects. 2. Life skills. I. Title.
BJ1581.2.K492 2011
248.8′6—dc23   2011019418

Author is represented by MacGregor Literary

Cover design by Christopher Tobias

11 12 13 14 15 16 17   7 6 5 4 3 2 1

Dedication
To people everywhere who feel knocked down,
may God lift you back up.

CONTENTS

ACKNOWLEDGMENTS

I would like to express my deepest gratitude to the faculty and staff of Columbia International University for their continued support and encouragement.

I also would like to thank the Nalepa Family, the Davis Family, and the Ferren Family for sharing their stories to help and encourage others.

Last, but certainly not least, thanks to James Lund for his help in making this project possible.

INTRODUCTION

If you've ever been on the scene after a violent car crash, you know how chaotic the situation can be. There are usually three types of people who respond.

First you have the witnesses. They usually want to tell everyone about what they saw. They know the facts and provide vital details. They answer the question, "What just happened?"

Then there are the law enforcement officials. Their job is to interview witnesses, collect other evidence, and process the information. One of their primary tasks is to assign responsibility. They're trying to answer the question, "Who's at fault here?" The police can then write an accurate report and the insurance companies can settle claims.

Finally, there are the paramedics. They aren't interested in the specifics about who did what. Their job is to find the people who need help, remove them from danger, and provide medical attention—immediately!

We all have unexpected and devastating crises in our lives. And just like the people who respond to a vehicle accident, we must pay attention to how we respond to our moment of trouble.

Some of us seek to understand what happened. Some of us want to communicate all the facts about the situation to others. Some of us look to assign responsibility. Some of us just want help. Any one of these responses is useful, but one by itself isn't enough. We must learn to combine them all, and more, if we are to effectively resolve disasters and get back on our feet.

This book can help you do just that. It is full of practical and time-tested guidance for meeting life's toughest challenges. No matter what catastrophe you're facing, it will help you decide how to respond in a way that provides fresh hope and strength.

Ready to stand up?

CHAPTER 1

BACK IN THE GAME

A setback is a setup for a comeback.

WILLIE JOLLEY

No doubt about it, life in the twenty-first century is tough. We're dealing with the effects of a recession that has cost jobs, taken away homes, wiped out retirement savings, and destroyed dreams. We're trying to make sense of new technologies that push us to always move faster, even when we don't quite know where we're going. We're attempting to build strong marriages and raise healthy children in an age where the future seems more uncertain than ever.

We sometimes feel like we're living atop an active volcano—the view is great, but we're not too sure how long it will last! We know that no matter how well things seem to be going, we may be just an instant away from crisis.

Have you ever had one of those moments where life punches you in the gut? I'm talking about times like these:

- Karen Sanders, thirty-six, loved being a stay-at-home mom. Then her husband, Matt, announced that he wanted a divorce so he could marry his new girlfriend. Karen is suddenly faced with finding a job in a crippled economy and raising seven children alone.

- Susie Rodriguez, forty-four, was ecstatic about her family's move to a new city and joining her husband, Gilberto, in a church ministry for youth. Then, one morning before church, Gilberto, who was employed but could not afford health insurance, suffered a massive stroke. Now Susie must care for Gilberto, raise two children, and pay $35,000 in medical bills on her $8-an-hour salary.[1]

- Charles Goodman, fifty-four, was a loyal power-company employee for nearly thirty-eight years. Then executives decided they had to cut back. Goodman, along with many of his coworkers, got the pink slip. After almost four steady decades, he's searching for work. "Right now is kind of trying," he says. "My kid is nineteen, and I'm competing against him for a job. Who would ever think?"[2]

If you picked up this book, you probably know exactly how these people feel. Sometimes, when you least expect it, life throws a roundhouse punch and floors you. And maybe you're thinking, *How do I get back on my feet? Do I even* want *to?*

If you've been knocked down too, I have a message for you: contemporary living does not have to mean feeling helpless and hopeless. I travel around the world speaking with people who are confronting sudden and unimaginable struggles: debilitating disease or injury; divorce; job loss; the death of a spouse, child, or parent; financial collapse; addiction; betrayal; and more. Despite their circumstances, many of these men and women have discovered ways to not just *survive* their crisis but actually *thrive* in it. I've seen them grow stronger from the experience. I've learned how they used the very experience that devastated them as a stepping stone to new beginnings, renewed relationships, financial success, peace of mind, and deeper faith.

Getting knocked down hurts. I know, because it's happened to me. Recovery after a knockdown is rarely quick or easy.

And it takes more than determination to get back in the ring.

Well-meaning friends will offer encouragement: "Hang in there" . . . "We're praying for you" . . . "You can do it!" Their remarks are sincere, but when you can't see your way out of crisis and can't find a reason to get up in the morning, you still need something more than uplifting words.

That's what *Getting Back Up* is about. It will help you identify exactly how you're responding to the body blow life just delivered. Once you've determined where you are, you can use this book as a guide toward practical strategies for useful solutions and fresh hope.

Ever hear the story about the man who was afraid to leave his home because of a premonition that something bad would happen to him? He resolved to stay on his couch and watch TV—and barely survived when a towering pine tree in his yard uprooted, crashed through the wall, and landed in his living room.

No matter how hard we try to avoid it, trouble will find us in this life. We can't control that. But we can reshape the way we respond to crisis. Comprehending what's happening to us, and then following a proven, effective method for dealing with disaster, is *energizing*. Mile-high obstacles don't appear quite so tall. Answers don't seem so elusive. We can go to bed at night thinking it just might be worth finding out what the next day will bring.

I've seen what a difference this makes in the lives of others. I've also experienced it in my own life; I've been knocked down a few times myself.

Let me tell you about one of them.

Trouble and Toast

My wife, Dawn, and I got married right out of college. We were both twenty-two. We had each other and not a whole lot else.

To save money, we passed on my idea for our honeymoon (flying to New York, staying at a fancy hotel) in favor of driving to an older condo on the coast. Then I entered graduate school, Dawn found a job as a secretary, and we rented a tiny apartment in Columbia, South Carolina.

A year later, things seemed to be going well, so we took out a mortgage to buy our first home. I earned my graduate degree and began my speaking ministry. Life was good! We even got a dog—Cooper, a cocker spaniel who was part bodyguard and part best buddy.

Then, on a day when I was in Colorado, Dawn faced an unexpected dilemma. On the way home from work, during the middle of rush hour, her old Pontiac suddenly died at a red light. She had to walk through traffic to a friend who, thankfully, was behind her. They literally pushed the Grand Am into a parking lot by bumping bumpers.

The car was a goner. We weren't ready to buy another, but with me starting to travel more, we felt we needed something reliable for Dawn to drive. Adding a car payment on top of the mortgage and other bills ended up creating a large leak in our life raft.

Since I was just starting out as a speaker, I needed to get experience wherever I could—prisons, schools, the YMCA, church youth groups. Many of them could not (or chose not to) pay for my talks. At the end of that first year of appearances, I added up my earnings and was shocked at the total: $2,993. This wasn't after expenses, either. I had grossed less than three thousand dollars.

Our savings account, which wasn't large to start with, quickly dwindled. Soon it was empty, yet the bills kept coming. We cut back on everything—eating out, clothes, trips to the movies, even seeing friends. It wasn't enough. We were in trouble.

Dawn is the accountant in our family; I usually don't pay much attention to our financial details. But I knew our situation was bad when she said, "Jeremy, I closed our savings account today. We just don't have enough to keep it open. All that's left now is the checking account."

I have a strong faith in God—plus, my degree is in Bible and biblical teaching—and I was praying hard for a solution. I know, however, that sometimes God's answer is for us to keep waiting and praying. Unfortunately (from my perspective), this seemed to be one of those times.

It finally got to the point where our cupboard was bare. For almost a week, we didn't have anything to eat for dinner but buttered toast. I remember looking at Dawn, chewing slowly on my bread to make it last, and wondering what we were going to do.

Sure, we could get a credit card, I thought. *But what good is that? We'd still have to pay it off, plus we'd get charged interest. That would just make things worse.*

I swallowed another bite. *Am I a bad husband? Did I mess up in buying this house? Is God telling me I shouldn't try to be a speaker? Why is this happening?*

I looked over at Cooper and his dog bowl. Even his food was starting to look good to me.

I have to admit here that I'm like a lot of guys—I don't like to ask for directions when I'm driving somewhere, and I don't like to ask for help with most other things either. I think it's a pride issue. I'm supposed to be the family leader and breadwinner.

In those early days of our marriage, I was bringing home very little bread, and I didn't want the world to know it.

When bills for electricity, water, and the phone came in and we had no way to pay for them, though, I knew time was running out. It was in my court to do something. Pride or not, we needed help.

The next day, I walked into our church and sat down with our pastor. "My wife and I are in deep trouble," I said, tears falling down my face.

He patiently listened to my story. Later, he called and said the church had a gift for me. It was enough to pay for the three bills we had due. Then a check arrived in the mail, along with a note saying, "Put some meat on that toast."

It was the beginning of a financial turnaround for us. The number of my speaking appearances gradually went up, as well as the amount I received for my presentations. Dawn got a raise at her job. Our "toast for dinner" days were just that: toast.

But you know what? I'm actually grateful we went through that rough spot. It taught me that a little humility can be a wonderful thing. It reminded me that God will guide me toward a solution if I'm patient. It allowed me to realize that everyone needs some help now and then. It gave me an increased appreciation for people facing their own hardships.

It also showed me that if you're starting to eye the dog's food, it's time to take action!

Are You Flat on the Mat?

I'm sure you have your own knockdown stories. You may be going through one such story right now. Not a lot of fun, is it?

Yet there are practical moves you can make to ease the pain and set you on the path to a fresh start. Your story might involve a sudden and tragic loss. Or maybe everyday troubles have left you reeling. Perhaps you're suffering from circumstances completely out of your control. Or *you* might be the sole cause of your heartache.

Whatever your situation, if life has delivered a haymaker, this book can show you how to make hay. The first step is simply to acknowledge that you're flat on the mat and you might need a little assistance getting back up.

If you can relate to any of the statements below, place a checkmark by it:

_____ *I'm so stressed that I can't sleep at night—but I can handle it.*

(Sometimes we act as if we're Superman and every problem is "no problem." But persistent stress and an inability to sleep are more than nuisances that drain your energy and ability to function during the day. They're also signs that something deeper is going on. It's time to check it out.)

___ *I'm overwhelmed by grief.*

(Everyone has their own theory about how and for how long to grieve after a loss. But you are unique. No one can tell you exactly what your response should be to something as devastating as, for instance, saying good-bye to a loved one. What you need most is a guide to finding the right response for you.)

___ *I'm busy every minute. If I don't have a task to do, I create one. I never relax.*

(We don't like pain much. In fact, we fill our schedules with all kinds of things in order to avoid it. But pain serves a useful purpose in our lives—for one thing, it calls attention to a need that must be addressed. Pain can point us onto a new and better path.)

___ *I blow up over the smallest things. I can't seem to control my temper.*

(Anger in itself isn't wrong. But unchecked anger takes us in directions we don't want to go. We may say things we regret or even physically strike a spouse, friend, or child. Anger also can be a sign of fear. If you're consistently or constantly finding yourself angry, maybe it's time to find out just what you're afraid of.)

___ *My life is pretty rough right now, but if God will just take care of (fill in the blank), then everything will be fine.*

(We all play the if-only game at times. *If only* God would give me that job. *If only* my husband would see how much his words hurt me. *If only* I had a nicer house. *Then* I'd be happy. But instead of playing waiting games, we can learn to start living, right now.)

___ *Everybody seems to think I have a problem. They just don't get it.*

(If several people are getting on your case about something that's going on in your life, perhaps it's not a conspiracy or that everyone's suddenly chosen to pick on you. It just might be possible that these people care about you and that a change is in order.)

___ *Sure, my life is a mess, but it's not my fault.*

(It's true: many of life's knockdowns happen through no fault of our own. But that doesn't mean we have to view ourselves as victims or wait for someone to rescue us. We can start on the road to recovery right now by reclaiming our lives and identifying our destiny.)

___ *It's all my fault. I don't deserve to have things go my way.*

(Are you on an extended guilt trip? God sees you as incredibly valuable and offers a way out of guilt and shame, one that leads back to a life of joy and freedom.)

___ *I used to have fun, but now I worry about everything.*

(Anxiety over financial circumstances, illness, failed relationships, or simply the fast pace of life can debilitate us and damage our faith. Two factors—laughter and trust—can help get us through. Both require making a conscious and continuous choice, and both strengthen us, allowing us to face the next crisis with confidence.)

___ *I have no energy. I'd rather just stay in bed all day.*

(When your view is blocked by fog and gloom, it can be awfully tough to see life with an accurate vision. When we discover how to rise above the clouds and gain a fresh vision, however, we find new energy and possibilities that stretch to the horizon.)

___ *I'll never forgive him for what he did.*

(Bitterness is like battery acid in the soul; it eats away at us, robbing us of vitality, peace, and joy. The antidote is forgiveness, which leads to freedom.)

___ *I've lost hope that anything will ever change.*

(Life's knockdowns have a way of stealing our hopes and dreams. Yet so often they're exactly the teacher we need to prepare us for transformation on the inside and for moving forward on the outside.)

Did you check one or more of the statements? If so, you may be flat on the mat in one way or another, and I believe this book can help you get back on your feet.

There are hidden opportunities in life's hardships and stresses. The Bible tells us that "in all things God works for the good of those who love him" (Romans 8:28).

Your knockdown is more than just an ordeal to endure. It can also be part of a process that leads to growth and strength for a lifetime.

CHAPTER 2

THE POWER OF PERSEVERANCE

*Success seems to be largely a matter of
hanging on after others have let go.*

WILLIAM FEATHER

Have you ever been rejected so many times that you didn't think you could go on?

When my speaking ministry began growing back in the late 1990s, I put together some resources for people to purchase if they were interested, including T-shirts and CDs of previous talks. But the thing everyone kept asking about was books. "Have you written anything?" they'd say. "You should." It seemed like God was trying to tell me something.

So I took ten of my best presentations and invested time and money working them into a manuscript. After considerable research, I sent out hundreds of letters and e-mails to publishers, asking if they were interested in my material.

It's a humbling experience to put your deepest thoughts on paper (or computer), send them out to the world . . . and see them rejected time after time.

Every day when I checked online or picked up the mail, I'd feel a surge of excitement. *This is it,* I'd think. *Someone's going to want to publish my book.*

But that's not what happened. Day after day, everyone said no. Most publishers weren't even willing to look at my manuscript because I didn't have an agent.

So I did more exhaustive research, and eventually I compiled a long list of potential agents. Again, I sent out letters and e-mails. Again, I felt that burst of optimism when the responses started pouring in.

Again, the answer was always no. And they wouldn't stop. Letter after letter, e-mail after e-mail, each a rejection.

What's wrong here? I thought. *I'm an established speaker. I have good references, a great education, a solid résumé. Hasn't God been calling me to provide resources to help people? Did I misread the signals? Am I missing something?*

I didn't think I could take even one more no.

The next afternoon, I retrieved the mail and took it into our kitchen. Among the bills and ads was another agent response. I almost didn't dare to open it. Yet, despite all that had happened, I somehow felt a flicker of hope.

So I tore the seal, pulled out the letter, and read the familiar words. Rejection again.

It was too much. I lost it. Standing there, near the refrigerator, the tears started to flow. Dawn put her arms around me as I repeatedly whispered, "I just don't understand."

I was ready to give up.

Stop the World, I Want to Get Off

It's incredibly difficult to keep pressing on when everything and everyone seems to be encouraging you to quit. When you're working as hard as you can and feel like you're falling further and further behind, it's natural to get so discouraged that you want to crawl into a cave and let the rest of the planet go on without you. Maybe you can relate to some of these scenarios:

- The single mom who comes home from work to find a broken washing machine, a stopped-up garbage disposal, a house that looks like the aftermath of a tornado, and two kids with fevers.
- The husband who works overtime and weekends trying to dig his family out of debt while dealing with a resentful and neglected wife.
- The employee who's repeatedly passed over for promotions.
- The dad who insists his sullen teens attend church, leading to angry exchanges every Sunday morning.
- The wife who's willing to work on creating a better marriage but has a mate who won't even talk about it.

Stormie Omartian, the author and singer, has endured more than her share of discouraging experiences. They began when she was a child and her mentally ill mother kept her locked in a closet. Her mother added to this abuse by telling Stormie she would grow up to be a failure.

Her pain did not go away with her marriage to producer Michael Omartian. Michael was critical and had a temper, which caused her to retreat emotionally. For nearly fifteen long years she prayed for her marriage and husband, most often with these words: "Change him, Lord!"

Finally, she felt she had endured all she could. "God, I can't live this way anymore," she prayed. "I know what you've said about divorce, but I can't live in the same house with him. Help me, Lord!" She didn't see any hope. She was ready to pack her things, gather her children, and begin a new life.[1]

Unleashing the Force Called *Perseverance*

When the daily routine of life wears on us—and especially when the unexpected rises up to knock us down—we need perseverance to keep going. According to *Webster's* dictionary, to persevere means "to persist in a state, enterprise, or undertaking in spite of counterinfluences, opposition, or discouragement." Those counterinfluences seem to crop up with annoying regularity. How is it that some people seem to overcome them while others wilt under their steady pressure?

Consider Thomas Edison, who built and tested more than a thousand light bulbs before actually getting one to work. Or Elvis Presley, who after his first performance at the Grand Ole Opry was told by the manager to go back to truck driving. Or Louis L'Amour, who received several hundred rejection slips before his first short story was accepted for publication. Or Michael Jordan, who was cut from his high school basketball team.

Perseverance is about more than repeatedly telling yourself to work harder and keep trying. It is an attitude, an approach to life that can conquer seemingly insurmountable obstacles. It involves patience, character, and faith. When fully formed, it's one of the most powerful forces you can unleash. And when life knocks you down, it's one of your most important weapons for fighting back.

Perseverance does not simply "happen," however. It is a trait that must be cultivated. You can develop and expand your ability to endure in hard times by adopting a few of the following strategies.

1. Look for the joy.

It's far easier to persevere when you enjoy what you do. Cal Ripken Jr., the Baltimore Orioles' shortstop who never missed a game in sixteen years, loved baseball. As a teenager, he received advice from his father that he never forgot:

> The secret to happiness is not in the money you make. It's in the quality of your work and how that makes you feel. So find out what you love to do [and] pour yourself into it.[2]

When you lose your job and are desperately searching for any kind of work, of course you don't have the luxury of pursuing your passion. Especially if the days drag into weeks or months, it's easy to get discouraged about the process of job-seeking.

Even in these circumstances, however, it's possible to find joy in what you're going through. Look for the silver lining. Does your suddenly flexible schedule leave you more time with your spouse or kids? Is this a new opportunity to exercise, clean out the clutter, or explore an idea for freelancing you've always wanted to try? Have you always wished you had more time to pray?

There is hidden treasure in almost any situation. You'll do a better job of persevering through your crisis if you focus on these opportunities and do your best to enjoy them.

2. SEEK OUT FRIENDS, MENTORS, AND ROLE MODELS.

No matter how bad your circumstances, someone has been through this before. Find people who can give good advice on what you're facing and ask for their counsel. If they had cancer, what helped them stay hopeful during the painful rounds of chemotherapy? If their child died, how did they handle the worst moments? Try to surround yourself with people who are known for their wisdom and steady, encouraging presence.

3. PREPARE TO PERSEVERE.

When you're fighting a tough battle over a long period of time, it pays to prepare. That's true on several levels: the physical, the intellectual, the emotional, and the spiritual. Let's say your mother has a stroke, and, because no one in the family has the funds to pay for help, you take on the job as one of her caregivers. Suddenly you're dividing your limited energy between your mother and the rest of your family. It's now doubly important to eat well, exercise, and make sure you receive proper rest. You'll also be a better and more confident caregiver if you read up on strokes and talk to the doctors about how best to treat and encourage stroke victims.

Likewise, you'll need emotional support during this stressful time. Talk to your spouse and friends about what you're feeling and going through. Plan regular times to download these thoughts and receive the encouragement of friends and family.

Finally, pass on your anxieties to God. Thirty minutes each morning of uplifting worship and prayer can prepare you like nothing else to serve others with a joyful heart.

4. Divide big jobs into little ones.

It can be overwhelming to think about getting out of debt when you owe thirty thousand dollars and are fighting to break even every week. So, *don't* think about that. Instead, set a realistic goal and divide it into small, manageable steps. Even if you save only ten or twenty dollars in a week, you're still gaining ground. No one lost fifty pounds, wrote a book, or climbed a mountain instantly—it happened a pound, a page, and a step at a time. Review your progress periodically to remind yourself that you're winning the fight, and remember to celebrate each milestone.

The ancient Greek writer Plutarch said, "Perseverance is more prevailing than violence; and many things which cannot be overcome when they are together, yield themselves up when taken little by little." Any huge success is actually the accumulation of a series of many small victories.

5. Turn doubts into motivation.

I was a decent student in high school and college, but not a scholar by any means. My marks at Columbia International University in South Carolina did not include a single A in four years of undergrad. I was still surprised, though, when, as I contemplated continuing my studies, one person actually pulled me aside and said, "You know, Jeremy, graduate school is pretty tough. It may be too hard for you. I think you ought to consider going in a different direction."

That was a little discouraging, to say the least. The more I thought about it, however, the more I realized I could respond in two ways. I could let this opinion turn me away from my dreams, or I could use it as motivation to focus even harder on my studies.

I chose the latter. Guess what, I finally got my first A's in graduate school. I was as proud as any of my classmates when a year later I earned my master of arts in teaching degree.

Sometimes well-meaning friends will say things that hurt and can lead you away from what you know in your heart you've got to do. When that happens, look for ways to make it work for you instead of against you. Another person's doubts can be your motivation to prove them wrong and double your determination and focus.

6. BE WILLING TO FAIL.

It's tough to keep going when every move you make feels like the wrong one. Whether it's an ongoing health crisis, failed relationships, or jobs that never seem to work out, continual defeat will wear down the most optimistic soul. If you're tired of trying, it may be helpful to remember a simple adage: successful people have more failures than anyone else. The reason for this is that people who take chances and persist and grow through their defeats are the ones most likely to find eventual success.

You may have heard of a man who encountered continual disappointment yet wasn't afraid to risk failing again. He suffered two business failures, the death of his fiancée, and a mental breakdown. This man also failed in his attempts at public office: He bid unsuccessfully for positions as state legislator, speaker of the state legislature, presidential elector, state land officer, congressional representative, U.S. senator (twice), and U.S. vice president.

Yet this same man was eventually elected president. He led the United States through the dark days of the Civil War, preserved the Union, and issued the Emancipation Proclamation. His name was

Abraham Lincoln. Many consider him the greatest of the nation's leaders.

Lincoln endured enormous setbacks, but he learned from his mistakes and persevered. You can too.

7. ALLOW GOD TO GROW YOUR PERSEVERANCE.

In a mysterious way, our troubles allow us to discover and develop reservoirs of strength and perseverance that most of us don't realize we have. When we lean on the Lord, He actually uses our struggles to expand our ability to deal with them. It's a process that leads us to greater hope and a deeper faith.

The apostle Paul talked about this concept in a letter to the early Christians in Rome. He explained that, strange as it sounded, suffering was the foundation of strength because it was the first step toward hope.

> We rejoice in the hope of the glory of God. Not only so, but we also rejoice in our sufferings, because we know that suffering produces perseverance; perseverance, character; and character, hope. And hope does not disappoint us, because God has poured out his love into our hearts by the Holy Spirit, whom he has given us. (Romans 5:2–5)

Take a second look at Paul's words: suffering produces perseverance, character, and hope. I'd prefer to find an easier way to acquire those qualities, believe me. Yet it's comforting to realize that my struggles aren't wasted. God uses them to make me a better, stronger, and more faithful person. I trust that God ultimately will provide victory over the obstacles of my life. I can always persevere when I focus like a laser on this truth.

My faith and trust in God are what allowed me to continue pursuing a book even after I was devastated by a six-year avalanche of rejections. After all those negative letters from publishers and agents, I prayed harder than ever. I also went back to people I respected and asked for their advice. The message I heard from them and from God was, "Don't give up. It will happen; you just don't know how yet."

The remaining option seemed to be to self-publish my manuscript, so that's what I did. We were thrilled to sell and distribute nearly seven thousand copies of *One Step Closer*. Then I targeted a few of the very best Christian literary agencies. It was now or never for my publishing dream. Less than two weeks after I sent off my materials, one of the top agencies responded with a phone call. That contact led to my first book with a real publisher: *Be Last: Descending to Greatness*, with Tyndale in 2008.

Stormie Omartian also relied on the Lord to grow her perseverance. She prayed and listened for His answer. She soon sensed Him showing her the sad life that she and her kids would face if she walked away from her marriage. God seemed to be telling her that instead of leaving, she should lay down her life in prayer for her husband.

This wasn't what she wanted to hear. Yet she agreed to begin praying for Michael in a new way. Gradually, those prayers changed both Michael's heart *and* hers. Her perseverance, her prayers, and God's powerful touch lifted their marriage to new heights. Today, after more than thirty years together, their relationship is stronger than they imagined it could be.[3]

It was Winston Churchill who once said at a commencement address, "Never, never, never quit." There is incredible power for change in simply hanging on for one more day, one more hour, even one more minute.

CHAPTER 3

THE HURT THAT HEALS

I have found the paradox, that if you love until it hurts, there can be no more hurt, only more love.

Mother Teresa

No one feels grateful for pain—in fact, as I mentioned earlier, we go to great lengths to avoid it.

And much of this is just flat-out wise. For example, when cooking, we wear oven mitts to avoid burning our hands. When jogging or hiking, we wear cushioned shoes or protective boots to shield our feet from rocks and other sharp objects. When we're outside on a hot day, we apply sunscreen or put on a floppy hat to prevent sunburn.

When something *does* start to hurt—say, we stumble and twist an ankle—we're rarely thankful about it.

But maybe we should be.

The many parts of our body have been individually designed to measure pain in varying degrees. The fingertip, for example, is so sensitive it can detect the touch of an object at only three grams of pressure per square millimeter of skin surface. Yet the same fingertip does not register pain until three *hundred* grams of pressure. It allows our hands to perform all kinds of functions without experiencing that unwanted "owie" sensation.

The cornea of the eye, meanwhile, registers pain at only point-two (0.2) grams of pressure. Why is the cornea so sensitive? Because the eye is extraordinarily fragile. If something gets lodged under an eyelid, it must be taken care of immediately or serious, even permanent, damage can result.[1]

Pain recognition, in other words, is one of the body's most intricate and essential systems. It warns us when action is required. Without it, we'd soon suffer from even greater maladies.

Tuberculoid leprosy affects its victims by damaging nerves near the outside of the body. Fingers, hands, toes, and feet grow numb. The nerves no longer have the ability to register pain. People in this condition often suffer from serious injuries. They cannot feel the intense heat of an oven burner or the sharp stab of a protruding nail. When their injuries go unnoticed and untreated, these people often develop debilitating infections.

Though we rarely think of it this way, physical pain is more than a nuisance. It has a positive purpose. It's actually a gift, one designed for our health and protection.

What about other kinds of pain?

The Benefits of Pain

Emotional pain can be just as devastating as physical pain—often more so. The anguish that results from emotional abuse, the loss of a loved one, a job termination, or a friend's betrayal can make us physically sick and so overwhelm us that we can barely function. I've been there, and I bet you have too.

A woman named Patty fakes one smile after another for friends at her thirty-fifth birthday party. She blows out the candles on her cake at the appropriate moment, groans as expected while opening gag gifts (a cane and bottle of Geritol), and laughs at everyone's jokes. On the outside, she gives the appearance of having a good time. Yet on the inside, her heart is breaking.

For eight years, Patty and her husband have attempted to conceive. They've tried a fertility procedure. Nothing has worked. Now it takes all her energy to pretend everything's okay and to keep from bursting into tears. She's angry, bitter, and feeling abandoned by God.[2]

Meanwhile, a woman named Danielle, age twenty-four, feels trapped in a nightmare. Her uncle molested her when she was four. Her father is in jail. Her mom lives from one drink and one destructive relationship to the next.

On her seventeenth birthday, Danielle ran away from her North Carolina home with a boyfriend who eventually abused her physically and sexually. For a long time, she didn't leave because she feared that he or his brothers would hunt her down and kill her. Finally she worked up the courage to return home, only to have her mother slam the front door in her face. In desperation, she turned to prostitution to support herself.

Danielle is more than miserable. She's more than scared. She suffers daily from searing feelings of rejection and agonizing emotional pain.[3]

What are we supposed to do with all this *pain*? For many of us, the answer is: avoid, at all costs. Danielle turned to smoking, drinking, and drugs to escape her anguish. She even dabbled in the occult. She was willing to do whatever it took to block the feelings and memories that tortured her.

Maybe you have your own escape routes. Eating. Shopping. Reading. Movies. We all have interests that take us away from humdrum life for a while, and there's nothing necessarily wrong with that. What's unhealthy, however, is using our diversions to avoid dealing with what's causing our hurt. As with physical pain, there also is a purpose for emotional pain: a signal to take action.

It's so hard to believe that healing is possible when we're experiencing deep pain. Yet patience combined with implementing a few important steps does make a lasting difference. The pain that results from trauma, crisis, and loss can be the turning point that moves us toward a better future. It can teach us desperately needed lessons about ourselves, the people around us, and our world. It can give us a new ability to demonstrate compassion and empathy. And, when we're stuck in a bad place physically or emotionally, pain can point us toward true healing.

I encourage you to consider the following steps designed to move you through—and beyond—the process of pain into growth and strength. You'll find they really do work if you give them a chance.

1. INVITE THE PAIN IN.

Dr. Mark Laaser once counseled a woman named Mary, a sex addict who'd had several affairs. One day in therapy, Mary began sobbing. Her entire body shook. Finally she stopped crying and said, "That was really stupid. I just can't let myself be like this." Mary had learned as a child that she needed to be strong and that tears were a sign of weakness. [4]

Many of us are programmed as kids to believe it's wrong to display emotion, particularly sadness. We grow up unconsciously determined to bury the evidence of painful feelings. When we suppress our pain, however, we create new problems for ourselves that show up in a variety of forms: anger, depression, sleeplessness, irritability, headaches, and more. Suppression affects our friendships and family relationships, often leading to isolation. It detracts from our job performance. It damages our self-esteem. It pretty much makes us miserable.

Rather than avoid or bottle up your tears and feelings of pain, I recommend that you embrace them. Yes, it will hurt for a time. Yes, you might feel that once you start crying, you won't be able to stop. It's okay. The hurt and the tears won't last forever. Crying is not about being weak or foolish. It's a natural process for women *and* men, and it's the way our bodies were designed to deal with intense emotions. Crying is an effective method for releasing your pain.

It takes courage to open yourself to your pain, but when you allow yourself to fully experience whatever is causing you anguish and grief, you are ready for the next steps that will move you toward truth and peace.

2. KEEP A JOURNAL.

Whenever you're aching or feeling emotionally overwhelmed, put down your thoughts about it on paper or screen. Recording your pain as you experience it can help you to understand where it's coming from, where it's leading you, and how to let it go. It also can give you perspective on your progress. You may, for instance, be going through a particularly depressing day. A glance at your journal, however, may reveal that such days are occurring less and less often, giving you confidence that your pain is temporary and subsiding.

3. Find someone to talk with.

Often the best way to deal with inner turmoil is to talk about it. Identify a friend, family member, or mentor who will listen without judging you or offering knee-jerk advice. Tell your story, and keep telling it if it helps you deal with the pain. Many times, putting your emotions into words and allowing a wise adviser to help you interpret your feelings can lead to surprising understanding and resolution. Just make sure that the person you confide in is someone you trust and has enough life experience to steer you in a positive direction if that's what's needed—and is someone who will keep silent if what you really need is a listening ear.

4. Allow time for numbness and grief.

If your pain is due to the death of a loved one, it's likely to be a long while before your sorrow will pass. Everyone has a different time-table for grief—don't let someone else's expectations bother you if they decide it's time you were "over it." In the early stages of an unexpected loss, feelings of numbness, shock, and denial are perfectly normal as well. They'll help insulate you from the reality of your loss until you're ready to accept it. Give yourself the grace to recover at your own pace.

5. Don't rush major decisions.

Pain and grief exert enormous pressure on our emotions. The midst of suffering is not a good time to make important and permanent decisions. What you're feeling today could change dramatically in a day, a week, or a month. If you must make significant choices right away, call on a trusted friend or family member to offer counsel as well.

6. BE OPEN TO EXPRESSING YOUR PAIN IN NEW WAYS.

Even if you've never tried it before, you may find unexpected relief through painting or through writing poetry, a song, or a short story. Volunteering may hold new meaning for you. Other hobbies can be a source of solace too. Don't feel locked into the old routine or feel guilty about considering new interests. This may be the perfect time to explore a nearly forgotten passion.

7. CHERISH POSITIVE MEMORIES.

Sorrow over a loved one's death can be eased by reliving the happy moments you spent with that person. It may take time before you're ready to journey through those memories, but reminding yourself of the positive experiences you shared will help you celebrate their life and appreciate your time together. Talking with mutual friends, looking at photos or videos, and playing favorite songs all are ways to remember and cherish a loved one.

8. SEEK PROFESSIONAL HELP WHEN NEEDED.

The passage of time, the support of family and friends, and our own best efforts aren't always enough to relieve the terrible pain that some of us experience in life. If this is your situation, there is no shame in seeking expert or professional help. Psychologists, therapists, pastors, and other experienced counselors can provide the perspective we need to move from pain to healing.

Danielle, the young woman who'd been physically, emotionally, and sexually abused, allowed friends to put her in touch with a woman who helped people escape the sex industry. That contact led Danielle to an intensive, faith-based program for women in need. Danielle put aside her fears and mistrust of others; she joined the program, and she graduated. Today she is married and pursuing a career as a hair stylist. Reaching for help was the bold first step she needed to take in order to leave behind her painful past and forge a new future.[5]

9. Trust God to bring good from your pain.

Those of us who believe in God often blame Him for our troubles and pain. "Lord, have I offended you?" we wonder. "You must not love me if you allow this to happen."

Patty, the woman who repeatedly tried and failed to have a baby, certainly questioned God's love for her. "Does God hate me or something?" she asked Lynn, a friend. "Maybe all that stuff about God loving us is really just a bunch of garbage."[6]

Yet God does not promise His followers a pain-free existence. Quite the contrary. Jesus told His disciples, "In this world you will have trouble" (John 16:33). The apostle Paul told persecuted believers in Thessalonica not to be "unsettled by these trials. You know quite well that we were destined for them" (1 Thessalonians 3:3).

––––––––

What, then, is the purpose of our pain from God's perspective? Is it just a cruel joke?

Not at all. God allows us to suffer and experience pain for our benefit. Once again, Paul is one of our best examples. This is a man who was beaten, lashed, shipwrecked, and constantly on the move to escape his enemies. He also suffered from an unidentified physical ailment, one he pleaded with the Lord to take away. Paul says the Lord's answer, however, wasn't what he was looking for:

My grace is sufficient for you, for my power is made perfect in weakness. (2 Corinthians 12:9)

Paul realized that his difficulty forced him to rely on God and His power rather than on his own abilities. Our pain is an invitation to do the same. Because God is infinitely more powerful than we can ever be, when we depend on Him, we find unexpected strength.

> Therefore I will boast all the more gladly about my weaknesses, so that Christ's power may rest on me. That is why, for Christ's sake, I delight in weaknesses, in insults, in hardships, in persecutions, in difficulties. For when I am weak, then I am strong. (vv. 9–10)

Patty discovered this strength in the days after she opened up to her friend Lynn. She thought about how often Lynn had comforted and demonstrated her concern over the years. She also thought about Jesus and His painful death so many years before—a loving sacrifice for everyone, including Patty. She began to see Lynn's care as a tangible expression of God's love. She realized that God really did love her, even if she didn't understand the reasons for her infertility. Her hopes for a child did not go away, yet she found a new strength to accept whatever the Lord had planned for her future.

God does not waste our tears. Once more, there's an important promise in Scripture that means everything to those who suffer yet believe and trust in God:

> We know that in all things God works for the good of those who love him. (Romans 8:28)

I don't believe God is the cause of every terrible thing we endure in life, but I'm certain He works with us and within us to bring good from our troubles. He may use our pain to help us become more compassionate, to introduce us to others in need, to prepare us for a new direction in life, to strengthen us, or simply to draw us closer to Him.

If we trust Him with our beaten and broken hearts, we *will* find the hope, healing, and love we all seek.

CHAPTER 4

FROM DENIAL TO RENEWAL

Denial ain't just a river in Egypt.

MARK TWAIN

Most of us are experts at ignoring the inconvenient facts of life. We like to pretend that we didn't put on those extra ten pounds over the winter, that we didn't forget to pay the electric bill, that we didn't call our friend a controlling wife behind her back.

Acknowledging these events can be embarrassing if not downright painful. Have you seen the cartoon featuring a woman whose head and arms were being squeezed through the wringers of an old washing machine? Under her anguished face the caption read, "The truth will set you free, but first it will make you miserable."

For some of us, denial is our way of coping when life knocks us down. Sometimes it lasts only a few seconds. Maybe you're running behind in getting ready for an appointment, and in the rush you lock yourself out of the house without your car keys. If you're anything like me, you shout "No!" followed by "I can't believe it!" You know the door's locked, but you twist the knob a few times anyway. You've already checked your pockets for your keys, but you go through them again. In other words, you're not quite ready to accept the reality that while you are *out*, the keys are *in*.

This kind of self-deception usually is brief and harmless. We all do it. It's a way of giving ourselves time to adjust to new and unpleasant circumstances. When life delivers a knockout blow and we choose denial as our ongoing response, however, it's a much more serious matter. Refusing to acknowledge the truth about the problems in front of us extends our misery and prevents us from finding appropriate solutions.

Our denials can take many forms. Have you tried any of these?

DENIAL OF FACT

The most obvious way to deny the truth is to lie about it. We might leave out certain details in a story, agree with another person's statement even though we know it isn't true, or boldly call a spade a diamond. No matter how we do it, it's lying. Used car salesmen are famous for twisting the truth, but they certainly aren't alone: "I had no idea I was driving that fast . . . I never heard you ask me to clean out the garage . . . I'd like to help with your fund-raiser, but I'll be out of town this weekend." People lie to avoid uncomfortable situations or to make themselves look better.

DENIAL OF IMPACT

Sometimes we admit that we're up against a tough obstacle or that we've caused one, but we try to minimize the damaging effect it has on us or people around us. The apartment dweller who repeatedly tells himself, *I'm behind on my rent, but business will get better—I'll get another credit card and make it up in the next few months* is in denial if there's no realistic reason to think his income will increase. The mother who for years yells at and loses her temper with her children and then says, "It's no big deal, they'll get over it" is ignoring the impact of emotional abuse. The alcoholic who says, "Yeah, I've got a problem, but it's not that bad, I can handle it" is deluding himself.

DENIAL OF DENIAL

Maybe the most dangerous form of denial is when we don't even recognize we're denying reality. This is the drug addict who's been kicked out of his home and is living in his car but convinces himself that he chooses to live this way and can quit anytime he wants. It's also the wife who's out every weekend cheating on her husband yet tells everyone (and herself) that she's just hanging out with a friend—it's nothing for anyone to worry about. It's possible to be so deep into denial, and so afraid of being exposed, that we begin to deceive ourselves.

The problem with denial is that the longer it goes on, the more we hurt ourselves and the harder it is to come to terms with the truth. Turning denial around takes a heavy dose of acceptance and a cup of humility blended with a spoonful of courage.

Tears of Truth

Zena always was impeccably dressed, but behind her fashionable exterior was a cold, bitter, and controlling person. She also had struggled with an eating disorder for nearly twenty years.

She hadn't always been this way. Her childhood and adolescent years had been idyllic. She'd earned top grades, joined the gymnastics team, was a cheerleader, and sang in the church choir.

Zena's life took a sudden turn, however, during her junior year of college. That was when one of her closest confidantes, her grandmother, died. It was also the year she was raped.

The trauma of those experiences overwhelmed her. Over the next eighteen years, Zena withdrew from life. She developed the eating disorder to numb her pain. She did her best to forget about what she'd been through, to pretend as if it'd never happened. But her unhappiness was obvious.

Finally, Zena heard a professional counselor speak at a conference. Something inside her said *Enough*. A week later, she found the courage to make an appointment with the same counselor and begin talking about her past. Gradually, one session at a time, the icy stares that made up her protective wall became melted tears of truth. She accepted that she needed to feel and then release her pain. After so many years, Zena finally began living again.[1]

A friend of mine I'll call Steven had his own struggles with knock-downs. He was a teacher at a Sacramento Christian school, while his wife, Pamela, was a registered nurse. Both were committed to God and to raising a strong family. They made enough for the two of them to be comfortable, but when their first child was born, Pamela gave up her job to be a stay-at-home mom. The family soon found its budget strained to the point that Steven quit his job as a teacher to pursue a career as a real estate agent.

As it turned out, Steven was good at his new profession and had good connections. In his second year, he earned more than a hundred thousand dollars.

The relatively easy money was enticing. Soon Steven was devoting himself to making even more. He dreamed about what it could do for him. He wrote out a list of goals he planned to achieve by the time he was thirty-five: a second house, a yacht, a Porsche 911, a BMW, and a plane; earning his pilot's license; and working no more than ten months a year.

Steven's focus centered increasingly on his dreams and less and less on his family and faith. Yet he refused to see what was happening—that he was replacing family and godly values with worldly status and greed. He lied to himself, telling himself everything was fine.

When a new friend named Rick started talking about an opportunity to generate even more easy money, Steven was eager to pursue it. The idea was to establish a high-class laundry facility. Steven, in partnership with his stepdad, would pay the start-up fees and oversee everything. Rick would sell them all the equipment at cost.

According to the figures Rick presented, supposedly based on his experience with previous stores, it was a can't-miss venture. Steven was so excited about the prospect that he didn't check out Rick's history, didn't ask for advice from any of his friends at church, and certainly didn't pray about it. He just wanted to sign up and get started.

The problems began early with schedule issues and cost overruns. When the store did finally open, it lost money. Steven had to work there fifty consecutive days because there were no funds to hire staff. He quickly found himself deep in debt.

The laundry operation wasn't Steven's only problem. Soon after it opened, he moved into a private office with a computer. Almost before he knew it, he was addicted to Internet pornography. Though he tried to quit and even prayed for God to intervene, he didn't ask for anyone else's help. He felt it would be too humiliating. Instead, he gave up and told himself another lie: *I can't defeat this thing. This is who I am.*

His mental and physical health began to decline. He ate poorly and couldn't sleep. He went into a depression and experienced anxiety attacks. He ignored or was short with Pamela and their children. He realized his marriage was falling apart, yet he still wasn't willing to confront his issues.

One December evening, Steven passed on the chance to go Christmas shopping with his family, saying he needed to catch up on work at his office. Pamela, hoping to have a little private time with Steven, arranged for the kids to have dinner with their grandparents and returned early from shopping. Her plan to surprise Steven left her with a shock of her own when she walked in and found her husband viewing pornographic images on the computer.

Suddenly, Steven had a choice to make. He could deny that he had a problem with pornography and say it was a one-time mistake. He could blame his struggles on his wife or the pressures of his financial situation. He could argue that looking at a few pictures of naked women was no big deal.

Instead, Steven chose to face reality. He had a problem he couldn't hide any longer. *This is out of control,* he thought. *I can't fix this myself.*

I need help. By putting aside his pride, allowing himself to be humbled in front of his wife, and accepting that he needed help with a serious issue, he took the first and most important step toward life change.

Acceptance Will Set You Free

Are you using denial to deal with a knockdown? Maybe, like Steven, your marriage is falling apart because of a secret addiction. Maybe, like Zena, your soul is numbed and warped because you'd rather not confront a past trauma. Perhaps you're ignoring the time you wronged someone else and the guilt is quietly making you miserable. Whatever the issue, know that you *can* move toward reality without it destroying you or your world. Acceptance, rather than avoidance, is a decision that can help set you free.

Here's a simple self-quiz that will help you identify if you're living in denial. Answer each question with a yes or no.

1. *In the last month, have I ignored the concerns of family or friends about choices I've made? (Y/N)*
2. *Do I use anger, accusations, or tears to change the subject when people bring up topics I'd rather not discuss? (Y/N)*
3. *Have my eating, drinking, or sleeping habits changed recently for no apparent reason? (Y/N)*
4. *Is fear controlling me in any way? (Y/N)*
5. *Do I believe it's unacceptable to let others see that I have struggles? (Y/N)*
6. *Do I find myself coming up with excuses for my behavior? (Y/N)*

If you answered yes to any of these, you may be allowing denial to poison your life. Please realize there is an antidote—a better way to live.

———

Either on TV or in real life, you've probably watched a court official swear in a trial witness with the following words: "Do you swear to tell the truth, the whole truth, and nothing but the truth, so help you God?" That's a pretty good summary of the process we all need to walk through when we're facing a crisis. Let me explain.

The Truth. Let's say your boss summons you to his office. "We've had a rough year," he says. "Our budget's been cut, and frankly your performance consistently hasn't been what we'd hoped. I'm sorry to do this, but I have to let you go."

You may be shocked—certainly you'll be dismayed—but pretending nothing has happened won't change things back to the way they were. You won't be able to hide it from your spouse, and you won't be able to pay the bills on imagination. The sooner you accept the truth that you presently don't have a job, the sooner you can begin taking steps to minimize the damage and find a solution to your crisis.

The Whole Truth. It's easy to filter out news we don't want to hear. For example, the temptation may be to admit that our job is gone while painting the future with an overly optimistic brush. If you're thinking things like *It's only a matter of time till they rehire me,* or *We don't need to cut back; I'll find a new job in no time,* you're probably fooling yourself. Accepting the whole truth means being realistic about what's happened.

On the other hand, attempting to turn your situation into an even bigger malady than it is also means you're avoiding the truth. Some people deny the positives that can result from unexpected trouble. For example: Is a better job waiting? Have you always wanted to try working from home? Embracing the whole truth not only allows for mistakes and circumstances but also involves giving yourself credit for the skills and experience you've acquired, recognizing the financial and emotional resources in your life, and realizing, again, that there's opportunity in every setback.

Nothing but the Truth. Sometimes we try to insulate ourselves from the pain of a knockdown by adding layers of lies. We might blame job loss, for instance, on a supervisor "who's never liked me" or "who's always been threatened by my ability." If we adopt "nothing but the truth," however, we might have to admit that, wholly or partially, it was our lack of performance that led to our dismissal.

So Help Me God. Facing the facts—the real, complete, and unadorned truth—of our situation can be intensely painful for a time. Even so, it likewise positions us to accept that we aren't necessarily strong enough to handle life on our own. The Bible says,

> I can do everything through him who gives me strength. (Philippians 4:13)

For people of faith, no resource is more powerful or assuring than God. If we're willing to put aside pride and admit to the Lord that we need help, we're likely to find the strength to move forward.

––––––

Often God puts people in our lives that can help us find the twisting path back to fulfillment and joy. For Zena, it initially was a Christian counselor, followed by a supportive therapy group. Zena eventually conquered her eating disorder and decided she was in a unique position to be an effective counselor on a rape crisis hotline. She found peace by taking the negative of her past experience and turning it into a positive.

For Steven, the turnaround began with "crawling back to God" and continued with his wife's steadfast support and encouragement. Steven and Pamela also began seeing a Christian counselor. The pornography ended, and their marriage gradually moved from denial to renewal. They still had to declare bankruptcy to resolve Steven's financial mistakes, but today he's back on his feet and happily employed as an instructor at his alma mater.

"None of that had to happen," Steven says of his past mistakes. "I could have made different decisions and done far less damage. But I'm so thankful for the growth and maturity that came out of it for Pamela and me.

"Even in my deepest, darkest pit, God was still there with me. I denied everything else, but I couldn't deny His love for me."

I recommend that periodically you take the self-quiz above. Denial is a destroyer that should be cut off as quickly as possible. Acceptance and truth *always* are your surest path to peace and freedom.

CHAPTER 5

TURNING ANGER
INTO POSITIVE ACTION

*It is wise to direct your anger towards problems,
not people; to focus your energies on answers,
not excuses.*

WILLIAM ARTHUR WARD

Tommy Bolt was a professional golf champion, but he was even more famous for his terrific temper. Huge galleries used to follow him on the course just to see what he might do next.

One day Tommy was giving a group lesson on how to hit a ball out of a trap. He called to his eleven-year-old and said, "Show the people what you've learned from your father when your shot lands in the sand." The boy picked up a wedge, then "hurled it as high and far" as he could![1]

Most of us allow anger to get the best of us at times—some more often than others. According to a "Boiling Point Report 2008" (sponsored by Britain's Mental Health Organisation), more than one in ten people said they have trouble controlling their anger, and more than one in four said they worry about how angry they sometimes feel. Sixty-four percent of respondents either agreed or strongly agreed that people in general are getting angrier.[2]

We know what happens to us physically when we get mad. Adrenaline floods our system. Our heart rate rises along with our blood pressure.

Our breathing turns shallow. Muscles tense, skin flushes, and temperature increases. We shift into alert status, ready to react to danger or threat.

We often hear about *road rage* and *anger management* in the media. From all that publicity, some of us have the notion that any kind of anger is bad. Not true. It's a perfectly appropriate response to cruelty or injustice (for instance). It also would be right for you to feel angry if an intruder invaded your home or if an unreasonable neighbor threatened your children.

Consider these examples from history:

- Jesus Christ upended the tables of the moneychangers in Jerusalem's temple courts, declaring, "Is it not written: 'My house will be called a house of prayer for all nations'? But you have made it a 'den of robbers' " (Mark 11:17).
- The efforts of abolitionists led to the passage in 1865 of the Thirteenth Amendment to the Constitution (which prohibited slavery).
- Outrage over the widespread use of kids as factory workers led to child labor legislation in the United States and Britain in the 1800s and 1900s.
- Anti-racism activists marched and protested, helping inspire passage of the Civil Rights Act of 1964.

Many of the knockdowns we endure in life make us angry. *Nevertheless, our bodies were not made to remain in anger mode for lengthy periods of time.* It's bad for our health—not to mention our golf games—if we stay mad for too long. The challenge is figuring out how to channel our anger toward constructive solutions.

Most people favor a single style of anger management. Check out these examples and consider where you best fit.

THE EXPLODER

Exploders are like active volcanoes—sometimes a little shaking is all it takes to produce a cataclysmic eruption. These are people who yell, break things, stomp, curse, and make demands when things don't go their way. The word *subtle* is not in their vocabulary; when they're mad (which is often), everyone knows it.

The exploder is quick to blow up and usually quick to calm down once the initial blast has passed. That can be good for his or her blood pressure, but the people around often feel as if they've been buried in a sea of molten lava.

The Victim

Victims struggle with expressing their emotions, usually because they were taught that anger is bad, so their anger remains bottled up and unresolved. Rather than showing their anger, they turn it inward on themselves. They smother their spirit through self-belittlement, blame, and guilt. "I can't do anything right" is a frequent lament.

Victims often suffer from psychosomatic problems: hypertension, headaches, and colitis. They may cling to others to the point of driving them away.

The Manipulator

Manipulators likewise hide their anger. They don't raise their voice or curse. Instead of turning their anger inward, however, they lash out at others with sarcasm, innuendo, and comments intended to inspire guilt. Manipulators employ any method that seems to work—authority, money, power, dependency—to get what they want, leaving those around them feeling used and abused.

The Rager

Ragers often were raised by controlling parents. As grownups, they're angry at the world, ready to attack on even slight provocation. Their perpetual fury pushes others away and leads to frequent disputes. They tend to see the worst in everything and everyone. And they attempt to protect themselves from hurt by making anger their default mode of operation.[3]

Any of these toxic anger management styles sound familiar?

If so, don't take shots at yourself. When life delivers a blow we never saw coming—a close friend's betrayal, a devastating injury, an undeserved demotion—it's easy to allow our anger to drive us into an unhealthy response.

Remember: *your anger may be justified. It's okay to be angry.*

Let's use that anger to fuel a constructive plan of action.

THE RELEASER

Instead of taking on the role of exploder, victim, manipulator, or rager when crisis strikes, I recommend another style: release. Releasers make anger their ally. Their approach is *feel it,* then *use it,* then *let it go.* They don't try to hide their anger or unleash it on innocent bystanders. Instead, they embrace their outrage and recognize it as a signal to adopt a strategy for positive action.

These are the steps releasers take when they get angry:

1. *Identify the source of the problem.* The releaser doesn't waste time assigning blame, attempting to shift responsibility, feeling guilty, or making excuses. The approach instead is to honestly evaluate what's happened and to ascertain what caused the crisis.
2. *Energize and plan.* Releasers know that anger produces temporary energy. Rather than try diffusing it or unloading it inappropriately, the releaser welcomes and fully feels the anger, then focuses it on the problem by identifying a plan of attack.
3. *Act on the need.* Once the plan is formed, releasers use their energy to put the plan into action. They also transform their anger into determination to implement future steps.
4. *Let go of the anger.* Hanging on to anger is unhealthy and destructive, both to self and to others. When releasers have done all they can to turn the crisis around, they release their anger, knowing they've turned it into beneficial action.[4]

For people of faith, relinquishing anger means trusting God to take care of the situation. Jesus said, "Will not God bring about justice for his chosen ones, who cry out to him day and night? Will he keep putting them off? I tell you, he will see that they get justice, and quickly" (Luke 18:7–8).

If we trust God, we don't have to assume the burden of making someone else pay when we're wronged or of fixing everything when something happens that we can't handle. "Do your best and let God do the rest" is more than a trite saying—it's a philosophy founded on ageless wisdom. It's much easier to keep anger in its place when we remember that God is in control and that we can trust Him to fill in the gaps we can't fill ourselves.

––––––––

Remember the (chapter 4) story of Steven and Pamela? When Pamela discovered her husband viewing pornographic images, she was furious. "How could you *do* this to us?" she said, her voice rising. "How could you hurt us this way?"

She began to cry. When she spoke again, she was almost hysterical. "You lied to me! I even asked you about this—you told me to my face that nothing was going on. We just had a baby together, and now you're doing *this*."

"I'm sorry," Steven said. "I don't want this life anymore. I don't want to be like this. I don't."

Though still hurt and angry, Pamela sensed he genuinely was filled with enormous regret. He was a broken man. She understood that returning the pain she felt with hot words and threats of divorce wouldn't solve the issue. Instead of *dwelling* in her anger, she *utilized* it to begin the process of repairing their marriage.

"I forgive you," she said.

Then her voice took on a businesslike tone: "This is what we're going to do. We're going to get counseling. You're going to get mentored. And you're going to find someone to be an accountability partner."

Steven nodded through his own tears. Within thirty minutes he called a trusted older friend, and within twenty-four hours they were on the phone with a professional.

Pamela's reaction was both understandable and justified, yet she was able to channel rage and woundedness into forming an action plan and beginning to implement it.

Her rage easily could have spiraled into destructive choices. She could have walked away from her marriage. She could have stayed with Steven and nursed her fury, making both of them miserable. But she focused her energy on the problem instead of the person and pursued a course that led to solutions.

The months that followed weren't easy, and Pamela dealt with recurring flashes of anger over her husband's past behavior. But her wise response to Steven's struggles with pornography allowed her to release her anger and paved the road to a restored relationship. Today, they enjoy a healthy marriage with three wonderful children.

We're not all natural releasers. And it's true that channeling anger is easier said than done. But you can *become* one, and you *can* do it.

When the steam starts rising, remember to pause and ask yourself a few questions. Here's a quick self-exam that will help point you toward becoming a releaser.

- *What am I really angry about?* So often, anger is a cover-up for another deep-seated emotion or simmering issue. Our manager yells at us . . . so we come home and yell at the kids about picking up their rooms. Sift through your thoughts and feelings to identify the real problem.

- *What am I doing with my anger?* Don't waste it on the nearest victim (even if he or she deserves it). Take advantage of your emotional energy, and, once again, use it as fuel for establishing a plan of positive action.

- *Am I staying focused?* When you're mad, the temptation is to lash out at anything that speaks or moves. Once you have a plan in place—a plan for facing your feelings and walking through your difficulty—stick to it.

- *Have I done all I can to solve the problem?* Sooner or later you'll reach the point where you've done your best to take care of the matter at hand. When you arrive at this stage, holding on to your anger doesn't help you; it just gets in the way of enjoying the rest of your life. Don't play the victim or the avenger. Be satisfied that you've responded to your knockdown in the healthiest way possible for *you*, and let God assume responsibility for managing things from here.

Covering Up Fear

One of the most common reasons we get angry is to mask another deeply felt emotion: fear. When you get laid off from a job or your significant other walks out of your life, the words that come out may be angry—"She has no right to do this to me!"—but the core feelings probably are closer to terror. You're unconsciously thinking, *What am I going to live on? How am I even going to make it?*

One of my best friends, Mark, experienced this kind of anger. He and his wife, Whitney, had a child, eighteen-month-old Jacob, who was their pride and joy. As many toddlers do, Jacob developed an ear infection. After two weeks, the infection seemed to be gone, yet Jacob remained lethargic. A visit to the doctor didn't provide any answers.

Two days later, when Jacob seemed worse than ever, Mark and Whitney drove him to an emergency room. Jacob was so weak he didn't even cry when the nurse couldn't find a vein strong enough to withstand a blood draw.

The stunning diagnosis was that Jacob had Type 1 (juvenile) diabetes. His body no longer produced insulin. The condition was incurable. Even more frightening, his life was in danger.

Mark couldn't believe it. He crawled onto the bed with Jacob to give him a hug, and then he began to cry.

Jacob was transferred to an ICU and hooked up to what seemed to be hundreds of machines. Doctors and other hospital staff began delivering a litany of information. Mark and Whitney's new reality would be filled with needles, blood sugar measurements, dietary restrictions, and doctor visits.

For Mark, it was too much. He was depleted mentally and emotionally. During a lecture from a nutritionist, he felt frustration and anger rising inside. *I didn't ask to enter this world,* he thought. *Now I'm getting a degree in the school of diabetes.*

The nutritionist droned on. Suddenly Mark stood, walked briskly to the exit door, and yanked it open. To his surprise, his pastor was on the other side, the man's hand held out to turn the handle that was no longer there.

Their eyes met. "I've been looking for you," the pastor said.

Mark stepped into the hallway with him and shut the door. Something told him it was time to let go of his anger and fear. He began to cry.

Mark remembers little about what his pastor said in that moment. What has stayed with him is the comfort he felt from his presence and his willingness to listen. It was as if the Lord had stepped in to give Mark a place to funnel his roiled-up feelings. He doesn't know what he would have done if his pastor hadn't been on the other side of that door.

"It was like God was saying to me, 'I know it's rough, but I'm going to help you through this,'" Mark says.

Jacob survived that first crisis. Despite Mark's initial resistance, he and his family have become experts on the many issues that surround diabetes. It isn't easy for them, but they are trusting in the promises they find in Scripture: for one,

The Lord is close to the brokenhearted
and saves those who are crushed in spirit. (Psalm 34:18)

Though there's no indication that Jacob's diabetes is going away, Mark and his family are encouraged that they have a loving, caring guide to lead them through each difficult day.

The next time you find that life has slammed you to the turf and you respond by ranting or raging, remember: *releasing* is much more likely to produce a helpful and workable outcome. Trust in your family, friends, and faith to help you focus, and then let go of your furious feelings. You won't regret it.

CHAPTER 6

THE BEST DEAL YOU'LL EVER MAKE

*A man of faith does not bargain
or stipulate with God.*

Mahatma Gandhi

If you're a parent, you've probably faced a scene similar to this one.

It's a hot summer day at an outdoor mall. You've just bought an ice cream cone for your five-year-old. He starts running around on the sidewalk with his arms outstretched, pretending to be a helicopter, the cone flying at high speed at the end of one "wing."

Sensing disaster, you speak up: "Kevin, I think the helicopter had better 'land' before you drop your treat."

Kevin ignores you, of course.

You warn him a second time, again with no change in the flight pattern.

Finally, the inevitable happens—Kevin bumps into a pole, the cone splats into the gutter, and the tears start to flow.

A few seconds later, you hear the question you knew was coming: "Mom, I didn't mean to drop my ice cream! Can you buy me another one? Please?"

You hate to see your child cry. You sympathize with him. But you're also on a limited budget, and you figure this is a good time for him to learn an important lesson about life.

"I'm sorry, Kevin," you say. "I warned you to stop running around. You'll just have to wait and eat something when we get home."

Then comes the kicker: "Mom, *please*! I'll be extra careful with the next one. And I promise, *I'll never ask for another ice cream cone again.*"

Despite his young age, Kevin is already a skilled negotiator. He has just launched into the phase known as *bargaining*. It's not a tactic reserved for children, however. As adults, many of us also try to leverage our way out of bad scenarios.

––––––––––

Think about it. When we're confronted with an unpleasant surprise, how do we often respond?

A police officer catches a woman speeding on a highway. "Please," she says, "I promise to be more careful from now on. Just don't give me a ticket." Or a boss tells an employee his position has been terminated. His first words are, "I'll take a pay cut, I'll switch jobs. Just tell me what I need to do to keep working here."

There's a couple I'll call Erin and Phil. They've been married eleven years and have two children. Their relationship, however, is in big trouble. Phil refuses to see a marriage counselor. He announces that he no longer loves his wife and moves out of the house.

Erin calls him repeatedly. She begs him to come back, tells him how much she needs him, promises she'll be nicer and pledges that things will be different.

Phil is cold. He repeats that his love for Erin is gone and says he's thinking about moving to another state. Erin doesn't know what to do.

The problem is, Phil has lost interest in and respect for Erin, and all her pleading only makes the situation worse. Desperate bargaining and promises of better behavior won't make Phil suddenly love Erin again.

Their issues are deeper than this, and Erin can't fix them by herself. She'd be better off confronting Phil and telling him she wants to work on the relationship. There's no guarantee this will restore their marriage, but it's more likely to earn Phil's respect and has a higher likelihood of success than begging.

Don't get me wrong. There is a place for bargaining and compromise. In a labor negotiation, both sides giving up some expectations in order to reach an agreement is considered a winning strategy for continuing a positive relationship. What's unhealthy, though, is when we misguidedly get locked into panicked bargaining to put off facing what must be faced. We see the road we're on, and we're determined to take a detour—even though there's nowhere else to go. It may be an understandable response, but it's also a surefire way to add unnecessary pain and delay entry into life's next stage.

Bargaining With God

When reality takes a tumultuous turn, we don't only bargain with the people around us. Sometimes things are so bad that we need a more powerful ally. Have you ever found yourself saying or thinking statements like these?

- "Lord, I never should have made that business deal. Now there's a chance we might go bankrupt. If you'll get me out of this, I promise to give 20 percent of my income to you from now on."
- "I don't know why I keep losing my temper. God, please help her to forgive me, and I'll start going to church."
- "Lord, you know that car accident wasn't my fault. If you help the judge to see things clearly, I'll read my Bible at least an hour a day for the next year."
- "My heart is 'not healthy'? My family needs me too much, God! I know I haven't been the most faithful follower, but if you heal me, I promise to dedicate the rest of my life to you."

People have been trying to make arrangements like this from the earliest days of our history. Egypt's Pharaoh struck a desperate deal with Moses . . . though he then didn't keep his word (Exodus 8:1–15). A man named Simon watched the apostles perform miracles and tried to buy their ability with money—though Peter turned him down and rebuked him (Acts 8:18–20). And on and on.

———

Bargaining *isn't* the same thing as asking God to intervene in our lives. It's natural and appropriate to pray for help when we struggle. Jesus gave us the model for this kind of prayer at perhaps His worst moment on earth, in the garden of Gethsemane on the night before His death. He said, "My Father, if it is possible, may this cup be taken from me. Yet not as I will, but as you will" (Matthew 26:39; he asked again in verse 42).

The Lord expects us to bring our requests to Him. Sometimes He gives us exactly what we ask for, which reminds us of His power and mercy. Often He has a purpose in mind that we can't see or understand, and the answer to our request is no. Our role is to accept His decision even if it isn't what we'd prefer.

Bargaining, an entirely different matter, is trying to manipulate the circumstances based on *our* abilities. Bargaining is an exchange, an "I'll do this for you if you do this for me" arrangement—and trying to bargain with God usually leads us toward trouble.

Psychiatrist Elisabeth Kübler-Ross, in *On Death and Dying*, identified five stages of grief people experience when they're diagnosed with a terminal illness or are dealing with a catastrophic loss:

1. Denial (and isolation)
2. Anger
3. Bargaining
4. Depression
5. Acceptance

Within the "bargaining" stage, Kübler-Ross described three elements:

- A prize offered for "good behavior."
- A self-imposed deadline.
- An implicit promise that no more requests will be made if this one is granted.[1]

Maybe you've seen someone in a tough spot, a family member or close friend, attempt to make just such a deal with God. Maybe you've done it yourself. This is understandable, and it even can be beneficial to the person doing the bargaining—as long as it doesn't go on too long.

We all need time to process devastating news. Bargaining is a temporary way to cope with what's happening. We're bound to be disappointed or worse, however, if we expect the Creator of the universe to negotiate with us as if He is a bartering salesman.

———

Joyce Landorf Heatherley has written about a woman whose husband died after thirty-three years of marriage. She wed again and enjoyed seven wonderful years with her second husband. Then they found out he had cancer.

The woman begged and bargained with God to heal him. When he was near death, she was praying on her knees at his bedside and heard the Lord's voice distinctly in her mind: *Your husband has prepared himself to accept death and to die right now. Tell me, do you want him to prepare himself for death again—later on?*

She opened her eyes and looked at his tranquil face.

"I knew right then I'd have to release him," she said afterward. "I didn't want him to go through that again—later on—so I released him. At that moment, a great peace settled over me. He died a few hours later. *Both* of us were at peace."[2]

If this woman had continued begging for the extension of her husband's life, her grief over his death likely would have been compounded by anger and pain. And then she would have missed what God wanted to do in their lives.

———

Landorf Heatherley also tells of another woman whose husband was dying. His doctor, in fact, said he was gone. Their children became hysterical, and they pleaded with their mother to pray for God to bring their father back.

The account doesn't reveal what promises this wife/mother made to God, but she did kneel down to pray. The husband/father opened his eyes, recovered, and lived nine more years.

Those nine years were miserable. He endured so much pain and unhappiness during this time that his wife regretted a thousand times that God had answered her prayer.[3] In this case, at least, the "deal" she struck wasn't much of a bargain at all.

It's All About Control

So, where does our urge to bargain come from? Much of it is a *desire for control*. When something rocks our world, it's easy to feel vulnerable and helpless, like a sailboat adrift in a hurricane. No one wants to feel they're at the mercy of circumstances. We'd much rather believe we still have some influence over what's happening.

A university experiment revealed just how important the perception of control is to us. Two groups of people, each in their own room, were given a puzzle to solve. Adding to the difficulty were a time limit and a series of distracting "background sounds"—doors slamming, bells ringing, babies crying, and more.

The difference between the two teams was that one was given a device allowing them to shut off the distracting noises, which obviously would make it easier to concentrate. The members of this team agreed to a condition, however. They promised to work as long as possible without turning off the noises. Only if the sounds became unbearable would they resort to working without them.

The experiment showed a dramatic difference between the groups. The team without the device failed to solve the puzzle within the time limit. One member even said it was "not humanly possible" to complete the task amid all the racket.

Yet the other group—made up entirely of humans, I might add— *did* solve their puzzle on time. Even more interesting, they never turned off the background noise. We can guess at the reason why. The members knew they could eliminate the distractions whenever they wanted, so they felt less pressure and stress. They perceived that they had control over their situation, which allowed them to perform better.[4]

Control is especially important to us when we face a difficult situation. If we feel we don't have any influence on what's happening, we're more stressed and more likely to handle circumstances badly. Nonetheless, no matter how awful the scenario, there are always some things we can control.

Let's say you're a single parent and your twelve-year-old daughter is in the hospital with a serious infection. The doctors are having trouble keeping it contained. Naturally, you're extremely worried. You love your daughter and don't want to see her suffer. You want this problem solved—*right now.*

In this situation, it's helpful to write down a list of the factors you can and can't control. It will help you to realize how much is still in your hands. For example:

What I Can't Control

- My daughter is sick.
- I need help because I don't have the medical knowledge to treat her myself.
- It's possible that the infection could spread and become more serious. Though highly unlikely (and horribly frightening to think about), it's even possible she could die.
- My insurance will only cover a portion of the medical fees. It's going to be difficult to make the payments.

What I Can Control

- I can ask the doctors for regular updates on my daughter's condition and more information about possible causes and treatments.
- I can do online research to learn more about her specific condition.

- I can ask for time off work to stay with her, encourage her, and let her know how much she is loved and appreciated.
- Since worry won't accomplish anything, I can adopt a positive attitude that will make me a more effective parent and advocate for my daughter.
- I can share my concerns with friends who can give me emotional support and may even be able to stay with my daughter when I need a break.
- I can ask my daughter's friends to visit and encourage her.
- I can meet with hospital staff to discuss our financial situation and examine possible payment plans.
- I can pray to God, ask Him to heal my daughter quickly, and trust Him to know what's best.
- I can resist the urge to bargain, instead relying on healthier responses.

Often, this kind of detailed reminder of what we can do in a challenging situation not only clarifies our options, but it also gives us a better perspective on how much we can influence what's happening. Regardless of what we're facing, the choice of how we'll respond is ours to make—always. That's a form of control that can't be taken away.

The initial petition of the famous "Serenity Prayer," credited to Reinhold Niebuhr, summarizes the approach we all can take in a crisis:

> God, grant me the serenity
> To accept the things I cannot change;
> Courage to change the things I can;
> And wisdom to know the difference.

What may be most helpful of all is to know that even when life seems to be spinning completely out of control, God has the matter firmly in hand. If you trust in His goodness and wisdom, you'll find it much easier to let go of the urge to bargain, leave your cares at His feet, and rest in the future He intends. That is the best deal you'll ever make.

CHAPTER 7

A MEASURE OF RESPONSIBILITY

Most of us can read the writing on the wall;
we just assume it's addressed to someone else.

IVERN BALL

If you grew up in a family with siblings, I'll bet you remember a few moments that went something like the following.

Little Johnny's at the refrigerator and has just poured himself a glass of milk. His younger brother, Fred, is bouncing a tennis ball in the kitchen at the same time. The family dog, Ralph, is under the table and has his eyes fixed on the ball, his head bobbing with each bounce. Meanwhile, Maggie, the boys' teenage sister, is sitting at the table, calmly eating her lunch.

Want to guess what happens?

Fred gives his tennis ball a little extra push; it gets away from him. Ralph, spotting his chance, launches for an interception. Ralph crashes into Johnny, who's walking with his milk. Johnny loses his balance and the milk splatters all over his sister. Maggie begins to wail as their mother walks into the room.

"Johnny just dumped milk all over me!" Maggie howls.

"It's Fred's fault!" shouts Johnny.

Mom isn't listening. She's already grabbing paper towels and wiping the mess off the table, the floor, the cupboards, and Maggie.

We all have accidents, many of our own creation and some much more devastating than this one. Our response to self-induced crises can mirror the scene above.

Some of us are determined to assign accountability for what went wrong. The problem is that, too often, we blame anyone and everyone but ourselves.

Others of us, meanwhile, jump right in to save the victims and take ownership for fixing the emergency. That's generally much healthier, unless we become so focused on helping those around us that we ignore our own needs and end up needing help ourselves.

It takes wisdom and experience to respond with just the right measure of responsibility in a crisis. Let me explain what I mean.

Rats and Bats

In his mid-twenties, a man named Paul Prather was on the verge of financial ruin. He'd dropped out of college during a deep recession. At twenty-two, he'd married his fiancée, Renee, who was barely eighteen. The only work the couple could find were minimum-wage jobs. Paul quit a minimum-wage job for one that paid half as much.

For the Prathers, it was a meager existence. The hood of their subcompact car was tied down with baling wire. Frequently they couldn't afford groceries. As bad as those days were, the nights often were worse. Paul sometimes jumped out of bed, grabbed a baseball bat, and fought off rats that invaded their kitchen.

The situation was desperate.

Paul had explanations for their predicament, however—lots of them. He blamed Congress for not providing better jobs. He said his bosses didn't pay him what he was worth. He complained about his parents never teaching him how to handle money. He even faulted God for not stepping in and providing a supernatural solution.

He had plenty of excuses for the state of his life, but none of them did him or his wife any good. After a while, his words started sounding hollow even to him.

Finally, he stopped condemning others long enough to look at the people around him. They weren't rich, but many seemed to be getting along just fine. *Maybe,* he thought, *they're doing something I'm not.*

It was a turning point for Paul. He hand-copied and memorized more than a hundred Bible verses about managing money wisely. He read books on personal finance. He cornered friends with money and asked them for their secrets.

What he learned was that he'd made a ton of foolish financial choices. No one had coerced him or pushed him into those bad decisions. He'd made every one himself.

Looking for the first time at his history without creating excuses was not fun. It made him feel like an idiot, not to mention guilty for putting his wife (and now their young son) through so much misery.

Even so, within that large dose of awful realization was a measure of relief. Paul finally was ready to take responsibility for his life. The good feeling from that day grew as he worked to reverse his bad habits. The Prathers' status didn't change overnight—it took ten years—but gradually they moved out of fiscal crisis into the middle class and then the upper-middle class. The blaming, along with the rats, was gone.[1]

When life knocks you down, playing the blame game only makes the situation worse. It postpones your ability to deal with what's happening by placing you in the role of victim. It's a way of saying, "I have no power or control over this situation; I'm at the mercy of people and circumstances."

It's true that you don't always have control over what happens to you—but you *do* have the ability to choose your response. And, if the fault really is yours, your best chance of turning things around is acknowledging it.

Pointing fingers at others also unnecessarily antagonizes the people who often are in the best position to help you fix the problem. A crisis is the worst time to push away your family and friends.

When you stop blaming and take responsibility for your choices and actions, though, you're likely to find that your obstacles aren't quite as impossible to overcome as you imagined. Admitting to others that, "Yes, it's my fault," is a way of reclaiming your life. It gives you power. It points toward solutions. It makes others want to pitch in and help you discover a way out of your mess. It's the first step into a better life.

Are you presently a player in the blame game? Here are a few simple suggestions to help end the games and get you back on your feet.

- *Identify your instinct.* When the car breaks down because no one's had it serviced in a year, what's your first reaction? If it's to finger the culprit, you're a blamer. Keep reading!

- *Temporarily eliminate your emotions.* Blame arises out of anger, frustration, and fear. Those are natural responses, but try to put them aside for a few minutes to consider your crisis from an intellectual point of view.

- *Be curious as a cat.* Ask questions and seek understanding. Be slow to draw conclusions. Gather as many facts as possible before planning your response.

- *Consider your culpability.* Ask yourself, "How did *I* contribute to this problem? What could I have said or done differently? What do I need to learn here?"

- *Take responsibility!* This means letting people know what you did wrong and apologizing when appropriate. In the case of the broken-down vehicle, maybe you assumed your spouse would handle getting it serviced, but maybe he or she assumed you would take care of it. It's your responsibility to speak up and clarify unspecified duties.

- *Seek a solution that works for everyone.* Does it really matter whose fault it is? What's important is figuring out how to solve the crisis and prevent it from happening again. If you can do that without assigning blame or alienating others, you're on your way.

Even if you've been playing the blame game for years, you *can* change your approach to handling traumatic moments. Start by rereading the suggestions above. Look at others who've earned your respect for the way they deal with tough situations. Be honest with others and yourself; you'll see that admitting mistakes isn't so awful after all.

Angel to the Rescue

Always looking to blame others for our part in creating a disaster is an extreme response. But it's also possible to swing to the opposite extreme. Some of us are willing to take responsibility for our own mistakes and troubles—and everyone else's too.

You probably know someone who's ever-ready to pick up *everybody's* pieces. When a babysitter cancels, a dog gets sick, a lunch is left on the counter before school, a job is terminated, or an eviction notice arrives, this "angel" comes to the rescue. Maybe you're one yourself.

That's wonderful . . . up to a point. The not-so-wonderful arises when you spend every minute taking care of the needs of others and never stop to recharge *your* batteries. Living this way feels noble, but it can easily lead to a new and more serious crisis.

Kathy Peel was a wife, mother, and devoted friend who spent her days running from meetings to appointments to kids' ball games to events. Whenever someone called with a request, she always said yes. Her calendar was completely booked. The longer this went on, the more overwhelmed she felt.

The day arrived when Kathy finally pushed herself too far. In addition to her responsibilities at home, she'd attended two community service meetings, cooked and delivered dinners to two new mothers, helped a friend highlight her hair, and assisted another friend with picking out and packing clothes for a trip.

By the end of the day she was so exhausted that she shut down and landed in the hospital. A battery of tests showed she had chronic fatigue syndrome. Suddenly, the woman who did it all for everyone was confined to bed and no help to anyone.[2]

––––––

Those of us who continually take on the responsibility of fixing all problems are particularly vulnerable during a time of tumult. If you live in perpetual stress and exhaustion because you're too busy to take care of yourself, you won't be ready for the next tornado—which is guaranteed to touch down sooner or later. And, if you make a habit of ignoring your own needs, you'll have twice as hard a time getting back up after life delivers a devastating blow.

How about it? Are you "Responsible Woman" or "Responsible Man," running around like a superhero with a big "R" on your chest? If so, it's time to reclaim your life. Review the following tips for bringing balance and speeding your recovery from a knockdown.

Learn to say no.

When the middle-school basketball coach calls and asks if you can help drive the team to their out-of-town game on Thursday, you may think, *Thursday? Let's see, I'm already volunteering at the elementary school in the morning, buying groceries for my neighbor on the way home, and attending a church committee meeting in the evening. Yikes!* But what do you say? "Uh, sure, Coach, I can fit that in."

Some of us are mighty reluctant to employ that small yet powerful word called *no*. We think it makes us self-centered and uncooperative. When someone asks for our help, we're honored to be invited. We usually *want* to help.

But agreeing to every request means we're unavailable or too wiped out to deal with more important ones later. It may cause us to miss out on taking care of a close friend or family member. It also may mean neglecting another important family member: you.

DELEGATE, DELEGATE, DELEGATE.

Moms especially may embrace the role of caretaker for their families. Making lunches, buying groceries and clothes, ferrying to and from school, picking up around the house, washing dishes and laundry—it's a never-ending job. Whether they enjoy or resent these tasks, thousands of parents daily devote hours to these mundane assignments.

It may happen at the office as well. Someone has to perform the little duties, as well as the big projects, that keep a workplace running successfully.

The issue, once again, is that a few of us are prone to taking on much more than our share. That heavy burden can quickly add up to burnout.

The answer is, *delegate*. At home, enlist your spouse and kids (nicely but firmly) to do their part toward keeping the house in order. For young children (maybe the spouse too!), make a chore chart and consider creating a reward system for jobs done well and on time. At the office, don't be bashful about pointing out what you're doing and about asking for help. A little assertiveness now will put you in a far better position to handle the crisis that's probably just around the corner.

RENEW AND RECHARGE.

Being a responsible person means recognizing your needs and incorporating them into your life. Have you ever taken the time to identify what they are? I encourage you to set aside a few minutes right now to record at least ten things that give you rest, renewal, and joy. For instance, they might be books, movies, coffee with friends, prayer, walks on the beach, hikes in the park, naps, swimming, cycling, sleeping in once a week, concerts, a hot bath while surrounded by scented candles, or just hanging out with your family. Whatever they are, you need to share them with your loved ones and include them in your lifestyle.

Don't stop there, though. Make an action plan for implementing your favorite habits. Schedule at least one to start today!

This might mean some juggling on your calendar. It definitely will require saying no to requests that come up when you've already planned for "me time." *Don't* give in to guilt. Your needs are important, especially if you've suffered an unexpected blow and are still reeling. This is the time to give yourself extra grace.

Some of your favorite "renewers" will be easier to install than others, of course. If shopping in Paris is on your list, you may need to budget for a while before you can turn that dream into reality. No matter—you can start saving for your shopping spree right now. If you commit and persist, it will happen before you know it, and the anticipation will be nearly as fun as the trip itself.

What's important to remember is that *you* are a priority worthy of respect and care. It's your responsibility to meet your needs so you can recover from the current difficulty and be prepared to manage the next one.

Even Jesus Christ established boundaries. Despite the suffering all around him, when crowds of people approached to present their needs, He "often withdrew to lonely places and prayed" (Luke 5:16). If the Lord temporarily set others aside so that He could refresh, how can we do otherwise?

––––––––

Either extreme on the responsibility scale—always trying to blame others for our mistakes or taking on everyone else's problems ourselves—is dangerous and unhealthy. The best approach is to find a balance. When we do that, we're in the best position to take care of the people we love, including ourselves.

CHAPTER 8

FINDING FREEDOM IN FORGIVENESS

To forgive is to set a prisoner free and discover that the prisoner was you.

LEWIS B. SMEDES

Bad things do happen to "good people." Just when we think we have life figured out, a friend rejects us . . . a spouse cheats on us . . . a drunk driver rear-ends us . . . we find ourselves dealing with rape, disease, or an eviction notice. It's only a matter of time until we end up flat on our backs, staring up at the latest catastrophe we never saw coming. And when somebody else causes our pain, we often have a hard time letting go of it.

Tom Bowers knows the feeling. He and his younger sister, Margie, were especially close while growing up, and they stayed that way as adults. At the age of twenty-seven, Tom lived with his family in Wheaton, Illinois, while Margie lived in nearby Oak Park. They talked nearly every night on the phone. During one of those conversations on a weekday spring evening, Margie told her brother how excited she was about her new job. They made plans for Tom to help her move into a new apartment the following day.

It was the last time Tom spoke to his sister.

Later that night, a man Margie knew casually from her neighborhood stopped at Margie's home. Thomas Vanda was looking for Esther, Margie's former roommate and classmate. Margie declined to give the young man any information. Suddenly enraged, he attacked Margie with a hunting knife, repeatedly stabbing her until she was dead.

The senseless loss devastated Tom. He felt overwhelmed with anger and a desire for vengeance. At Vanda's trial a year later, he sat directly behind the defendant and fantasized about what it would be like to stretch out his arms and strangle the man.

Vanda was convicted and sentenced to three consecutive life sentences without parole. When the sentence was announced, Tom watched the murderer shrug his shoulders and smirk.

As the days and years passed, Tom couldn't get over Margie's death. He was haunted by memories and thoughts of the future that Vanda had denied his sister. He dreamed of being with Margie that night, of taking the knife away, and of using it on Vanda instead.

Tom's anger sometimes made him physically sick. He had descended into the twilight zone called *bitterness*.[1]

Compounded Suffering

When another person leaves us with a devastating hurt, it's understandable to respond with bitterness. And, it's easy to justify. The other person clearly is in the wrong. We want him or her to suffer and be held accountable. What we don't consider is how much *we* suffer in the process.

Most of us don't become bitter immediately. At first, when someone betrays or harms us, we feel wounded. We search for a way to deal with the pain, which often leads to self-pity. We may ask ourselves, "What did I do to deserve this?"

If these kinds of questions last long enough, we move into seething anger. Our blood pressure rises. We replay in our minds the incident that brought on our pain. Though our desire is to take out our rage on the offender, instead it often poisons all our other relationships.

Finally, if left to fester, anger transforms into bitterness. We're plagued by a continual desire to turn our fury into revenge. We grow discouraged and disillusioned. Our emotion spills over onto those closest to us. We feel exhausted, joyless, and isolated. Our goals and dreams begin to seem meaningless. Life takes on a dreary tinge.

When we're down and hurting, bitterness compounds our suffering. It strands us at our point of pain and blocks us from the life we were meant to live.

Are you bitter about recent misfortunes, or about incidents from years past? Are you holding on to anger over someone else's seemingly unpunished sin? If the answer is yes, they still have a hold on you.

The solution for breaking free is both basic and very difficult to do: forgive.

Six Steps to Forgiveness

I know, I know. The idea sounds outrageous. Maybe you're thinking, *You don't know what he did to me. I can't* ever *forgive him for* that.

Before you toss this book into the fireplace, though, let me just point out a couple things. To forgive does *not* mean to forget. Further, it doesn't mean you're excusing someone for their offense. Rather, *forgiveness is instead a statement that you're through with letting someone else traumatize you.*

David Allen has described the inner turmoil that results from bitterness:

> Whatever the causes of our injuries, if we do not work through them, the hurt begins to harden our hearts. The hardness contaminates us. We are less able to feel and touch and make connection with others. In other words, the resentment and hurt in our heart produces alienation within ourselves and also alienation from those around us. Lack of forgiveness destroys relationships, increases the isolation and fragmentation in our world . . . forgiveness is essential to the healing of the heart.[2]

If that's not enough reason to forgive, I'll give you one more: it's spiritual. Our ability to partake in God's forgiveness is tied up in our willingness to forgive others. The Bible says, "If you hold anything against anyone, forgive him, so that your Father in heaven may forgive you your sins" (Mark 11:25). The Lord isn't out to punish us by asking us to forgive. He knows that forgiveness is the pathway to freedom.

Perhaps you're convinced and you're ready to give forgiveness a try. Where do you start? I recommend six proven steps.

1. Admit feeling hurt, angry, and bitter.

Sometime we try to pretend that when someone wounds us, it's no big deal. We'd prefer to smile through our days and forget about it. The problem is, we don't forget. The injury nags at us like a virus that seems like it will never completely go away.

We usually know when we're feeling guilty, disappointed, or hurt. Bitterness can be much harder to recognize, though; it develops gradually, so we may not even be aware of it. Ask yourself if you're suffering from any of these signs:

- Do I have trouble sleeping because of anger?
- Do I fantasize about getting revenge on someone?
- Am I obsessed with seeing that justice is done?
- Do I keep replaying a painful incident in my mind?
- Am I finding it harder to get along with people?
- Have I gradually lost enthusiasm for life since the moment someone hurt me?

Be honest with yourself. If you said yes to any of the above, you may have an issue with bitterness. Admitting the truth is the first step to letting go.

2. TALK IT OUT.

Some of the most difficult hurts to forgive are those done to us by someone with whom our relationship is ongoing. I know of a woman who had a baby that lived only a few days. The grieving mother was doubly wounded, however, when her parents decided not to attend the baby's funeral service. The message she received from her parents was that she and her baby were not important to them, and that because the baby had such a short life, it was hardly worth making all the fuss about a funeral.

Though terribly pained, the daughter did eventually sit down with her parents to discuss what had happened. Without launching into an attack, she explained her feelings and invited them to do the same. She learned that they hated to see their daughter so sad and thought going to the funeral would encourage her to mourn excessively. For the daughter, those words didn't erase the hurt, but they did offer a glimmer of insight that eventually led her to forgive her parents.

Here are a few suggestions for talking it out with someone who's wounded you:

- Share your hurt, and let the other person see your heart.
- In a calm voice, explain how the hurt has affected you.
- Don't accuse, attack, insult, belittle, or use sarcasm.
- Use positive statements whenever you can.
- Use "I" statements, like "I feel hurt because . . ."
- Avoid "you" statements, like "You are the one who . . ."
- Stay on the subject.
- Maintain eye contact.
- Try to talk about your anger without acting it out.
- Listen to the other person's viewpoint.
- Don't interrupt.
- Speak as though God is listening (He is).

Talking about your hurt may not be comfortable, but it's especially important if you want to restore the relationship with your family member, friend, or coworker. Even if you don't arrive at understanding or forgiveness right away, you'll feel better because you expressed your feelings.

3. Remember why forgiveness is necessary.

If we're wallowing in bitterness, we've probably lost sight of the nasty, selfish, thoughtless deeds we've committed ourselves. The truth is, we all are in need of forgiveness. We offend others when we wrong them or treat them carelessly. We also offend God.

The Lord doesn't want us to carry around this burden. He doesn't want to see us in pain. He knows we need to forgive and be forgiven. What's amazing is that He's always waiting and willing to forgive.

> If we confess our sins, [God] is faithful and just and will forgive us our sins. (1 John 1:9)

Accepting God's forgiveness and forgiving others are like two sides of the same coin. If Jesus could forgive the Roman soldiers and all of humanity for taking His life on the cross, can't we find it in our hearts to forgive the mistakes and hurtful actions of those around us?

4. Choose forgiveness.

If our approach to another person's offense is that we'll forgive when we feel ready, know this: it will never happen. Forgiveness isn't a feeling but a decision of the will. The feeling comes after we make the decision—maybe just a moment later, or maybe years later. It takes time for us to work through our anger and resentment. Our choice to forgive is a way of saying, "Lord, I am so hurt right now. I don't want to forgive _____, but I know you want me to. I am choosing to forgive and trusting you to change my heart."

Corrie ten Boom and her sister, Betsie, had been prisoners at the Ravensbrück concentration camp operated by the Nazis during World War II. Though Corrie survived the horror of her time there, Betsie did not.

It was two years after the end of the war, at a church in Munich, as Corrie ten Boom had finished giving a talk about God's forgiveness, that she saw a heavyset man, dressed in a gray overcoat, his hands clutching a brown felt hat, coming forward.

In the next instant, however, she recognized him, and she visualized him in much different attire: a blue uniform, a leather crop swinging from his belt, a visored cap with skull and crossbones. He had been one of the cruelest guards at Ravensbrück.

Suddenly, she stood face-to-face with one of her former captors. The man clearly did not remember her. He explained that he'd been a guard, "but since that time, I have become a Christian," he said. "I know that God has forgiven me for the cruel things I did there, but I would like to hear it from your lips as well. Fräulein"—his right hand thrust forward—"will you forgive me?"

For a few seconds, she wrestled with the most difficult thing she'd ever had to do. Her blood froze. She did not want to forgive this man for the terror he'd inflicted, for contributing to the excruciating death of her sister and so many, many others. Nonetheless, she was just as certain that she had to.

Jesus, help me! she prayed. *I can lift my hand. I can do that much. You supply the feeling.*

Mechanically, her hand rose and grasped the other. Then an amazing thing happened. A current seemed to race through her, flooding her body with healing warmth. Tears filled her eyes.

"I forgive you, brother!" Corrie ten Boom cried. "With all my heart."[3]

If each of us can find the will to *choose* forgiveness, we can trust God to take care of the rest.

5. PUT THE HURT BEHIND YOU.

I've read that the mind can record up to eight hundred memories per second and store the most significant of those memories for a lifetime. This means it's highly improbable that we can even learn to "forgive and forget." However, forgetting isn't required for healing or for forgiveness. What's needed is the decision to stop reliving the painful moments in our past.

Several years ago, a woman wrote about her husband of two years having an affair with a young widow, who then carried his child. The wife was devastated and angry. She wanted to kill her husband and the woman. She knew, though, that this wasn't the answer to her troubles. Instead, she prayed about her dilemma and found the strength to forgive.

The baby was born in the home of the husband and wife and raised as their own. He turned out to be their only child. In fifty years, the couple never discussed the incident again. "But," she wrote, "I've read the love and gratitude in his eyes a thousand times."[4]

Ken Sande, author of *The Peacemakers*, lists four promises we must keep if we are to put our pain behind us:

- I will no longer dwell on this incident.
- I will not bring up this incident again and use it against you.
- I will not talk to others about this incident.
- I will not allow this incident to stand between us or hinder our relationship.[5]

6. BE PATIENT WITH THE PROCESS.

In any close, long-term relationship, it's almost inevitable that the other person is going to hurt you multiple times with careless things they do or say. That makes forgiveness for the "biggies" extra tough. You have to enter the cycle of hurt, forgiveness, and trust over and over, and *that* requires time and patience. You may need to remind yourself that forgiveness is a process, that it's vital to your well-being, and that even though the results are not always instantaneous, it does work.

You may also want to remember that relationships restored through the process of giving and receiving forgiveness actually can grow more durable. It's like a cherished vase that's broken into pieces and then glued back together. The vase may show a few cracks, but in fact it's stronger than it was before.[6]

Peace at Last

Remember Tom Bowers, the man whose sister was murdered? He was trapped in a state of anger and bitterness for a decade. Then he ran into Esther, Margie's former roommate. He discovered that because Thomas Vanda had been looking for Esther, she had blamed herself for Margie's death.

"Esther," Tom said, "it wasn't your fault. Margie may not be here to forgive you, but I am. I forgive you on her behalf."

Later, Tom was preparing to teach a lesson for an adult Sunday school class. The theme was forgiveness. Suddenly, a voice spoke in his mind: *So, you plan to teach about forgiveness? When are* you *going to forgive?*

Tom realized in a moment that rage and bitterness were destroying his life. He had to make a choice. One day, soon after, he knew it was time. "Thomas Vanda, I forgive you," he said aloud. He repeated the words over and over: "Thomas Vanda, I forgive you." As he did, he felt a burden lift. In its place was an overwhelming sense of peace.[7]

You too can find peace and freedom if you make the difficult but lifesaving choice to forgive.

CHAPTER 9

LETTING GO OF GUILT

Guilt is the very nerve of sorrow.

HORACE BUSHNELL

After being out of town, it's always a joy to come home and be welcomed with excited hugs from my boys: Jaden, ten, and Dylan, four. That was the scene recently after I returned from a cross-country trip. Jaden added to his enthusiastic greeting by proudly informing me, "Dad, I got you an A&W Root Beer from Grandma's house!"

My parents, who live nearby, keep a variety of delicious sodas and fruit drinks in their garage refrigerator specifically for their grandsons. After all, it's their job to spoil my kids. Not long before, Jaden had raided their supply not only for himself but also on my behalf. It was so nice of him to think of me. Sure enough, when I opened our fridge, I spotted two root beers side by side on the shelf, so I took mine and enjoyed it.

One late evening, a couple days later, I was back at the fridge again. I'd had a long day of work and meetings. I was tired and ready for a little bedtime snack. Hoping to find something quick and tasty, I opened the door. Right away, my eyes were drawn to a lone can of root beer. My hand went out, and before I knew it the contents were gone. What I'd forgotten was that I'd already downed the one intended for me. This was Jaden's.

The next morning, it wasn't long before a surprised and sad wail filled the air: "Hey, what happened to the A&W I got at Grandma's? Dad, did you drink my root beer?"

As soon as I heard Jaden's voice, I knew I'd made a big mistake. Guilt has been described as a sense of remorse for past emotions, thoughts, or actions. That's exactly what I was feeling as I looked into the disappointed eyes of my boy.

"Jaden, I'm really sorry," I said. "It looks like we might have to make another trip to Grandma's."

We all go on guilt trips from time to time, often with a little encouragement from someone we love ("You're the only daughter I have, so how come you never visit me?"). Most of these moments are relatively minor and easy to resolve. I was disappointed in myself for forgetting about and drinking Jaden's root beer, but once I apologized and we got him a new one, I didn't continue to dwell on it.

Sometimes, however, our encounters with guilt create ripples that extend far into the future. These can bring us to our knees, creating more damage than the incident that inspired the guilt in the first place. If you're experiencing this kind of guilt, it's indescribably important that you deal with it before it takes over your life and completely steals your joy. Whether you're anguishing over a careless insult, a forgotten and broken promise, or an intentional offense, unresolved guilt can take you down and pin you to the mat until you take the necessary steps to get back on your feet.

A New and Hope-Filled Life

Guilt torments us in many ways. Rick Warren says that, for example, it can create distorted motivations:

> Many people are driven by guilt. They spend their entire lives running from regrets and hiding their shame. Guilt-driven people are

manipulated by memories. They allow their past to control their future. They often unconsciously punish themselves by sabotaging their own success.[1]

People overwhelmed by guilt tend to struggle with keeping their lives balanced. They frequently take on too many tasks, feel responsible for fixing others' problems, and can be acutely aware of when the people around them are in pain. They may suffer from a continual sense of loss or be hypersensitive. They also might become immobilized and have difficulty making decisions.

Guilt is like a poison that seeps into everything we think and do, slowly draining our life away.

We don't need to keep suffering from regret and remorse, though. It's possible to move beyond our mistakes, along with the ones we perceive we've made, and start a new, hope-filled life.

Are you plagued by any of the symptoms described above? Do you know that you struggle with guilt? Have you been wrestling with guilt without even realizing it? Are you ready to put an end to your emotional turmoil?

If guilt has you feeling like a prisoner, let's see if we can set you free. The following series of questions will help you identify the source of your guilt and guide you toward a more joy-filled existence.

DO I HONESTLY HAVE REASON TO FEEL GUILTY?

Mary Alice and her husband had long made parenting one of their top priorities. Two of their three daughters grew up as wonderful examples of a nurturing family environment. The third, however, was constant trouble before she ran off at age eighteen with a convict who'd already been married three times.

Mary Alice was consumed with guilt. "I thought I would go around forever with FAILURE branded on my forehead," she said. "My husband and I had long discussions about whether we should drop out of the church and not attempt to minister to others because of our failure."[2]

Sometimes you do all the right things, and the situation still turns out badly. Though you may figure that somehow you must be to blame, it's simply not true. We're not responsible for the wrong decisions other people make. If we've taught them correctly, that even includes our own children.

Victims of physical, sexual, and emotional abuse, as well as of violent crimes, are especially prone to low self-esteem and to feeling responsible for and guilty over what happened to them. If this is part of your history, I strongly encourage you to talk with a professional counselor. If you wonder whether you're blaming yourself for a mistake made by someone else, I urge you to think about this for a while—a long while. Remind yourself daily that you aren't responsible for the choices of others. This is the first step toward letting go of the guilt.

Have I fully confessed my mistakes?

Partially confessing a bad decision likely will lead to guilt. Maybe you've admitted to your spouse that you spent "more than you should have" while shopping for Christmas presents online. You neglected to mention, however, that it was *three thousand dollars* more, and it's going to be mighty hard to make the mortgage payment next month.

You probably can guess how to solve this one—it's time to fully 'fess up. The sooner you open up about all the gory details of your transgressions, no matter how awful, the sooner you'll be able to release your guilt and begin dealing with the crisis you've created. For people of faith, this means telling everything not only to the person you've offended but also to God. He already knows what we're trying to hide; it's the process of admitting it that leads to our freedom.

> He who conceals his sins does not prosper,
> but whoever confesses and renounces them finds mercy.
> (Proverbs 28:13)

Have I asked for forgiveness?

Maybe you've gossiped about a former friend, saying that you think she's having an affair. You're starting to hear other people repeat the rumor *you* started and are realizing you messed up. To get rid of the guilt (and because it's the right thing to do), you go to her, swallow a couple of times, and admit you're responsible for the vicious rumor.

That's a good response to your mistake, but you still have work to do. Though you'd probably like to get out of the conversation as quickly as possible, you need to take it a step further or your conscience will still eat at you. You need to ask for her forgiveness.

She may not give it to you. She may explode in anger, throw things at you, or start spreading a few rumors of her own about you. None of that would be very fun, but you're not responsible for her response. The important thing is to give her the opportunity to forgive you. If she takes it, it will alleviate any potential bitterness on her part. Either way, it will mean you've made the effort and are ready to move past your guilt.

Still, you're not quite done. As we saw in chapter 8, if you believe in God, you must ask for His forgiveness as well. Though you'll feel better if you ask the person you've offended to forgive you, that's really for their benefit. *God* always offers total forgiveness, and He's the only one who can sweep your mistakes so far away that it's as if they never occurred.

> As far as the east is from the west,
> so far has he removed our transgressions from us.
> (Psalm 103:12)

That's especially comforting to know when the person we've hurt is no longer living. We can still find relief from our guilt if we seek forgiveness from our Creator.

Is my repentance genuine?

If a colleague comes up to you and says, "Hey, I'm sorry about interrupting you in front of the boss at the meeting this morning—I hope you'll forgive me," but then does the same thing the next day, his repentance over his behavior probably isn't genuine. It's entirely possible to say the words and not mean them. If we confess our mistakes without regret or without any interest in changing our attitude and our actions, guilt will remain lodged in our lives.

Most people regret putting others in painful situations. If that's not always true for you, you may need a lesson in empathy. Look at the situation from the other person's point of view. Imagine how you'd feel if you'd been the victim of your poor behavior. Make a serious effort to think less about yourself and more about the needs and desires of the people around you, and you'll begin to develop sincere repentance.

Have I tried to make things right with the people I've hurt?

You can admit your wrongdoing to someone, humbly vow to change your ways, and still be ensnared by guilt. The problem may be that you haven't stepped forward to make things right.

Remember our example of the former friend maligned by your gossip? You must do more than confess and ask for forgiveness. You also need to go to the people you spoke to earlier and tell *them* about your mistake.

This principle applies to more than just reputations. If it's in your power to fix the matter and you want to rid yourself of guilt, jump up and get it done. You'll sleep better immediately.

Am I willing to forgive myself?

Elaine was sixteen when she became pregnant. Overwhelmed by shame and by her parents' disapproval, she chose to have an abortion. For Elaine, though, the emotional trauma was only beginning. She carried a heavy burden of guilt over the abortion into her eventual marriage with a man named Steve. It strained their relationship. Their inability to have children intensified Elaine's guilt.

What was I thinking? she pondered. *I killed my child. I threw away the only chance I'll ever have for a son or daughter. How could I have been so blind? What will I tell my precious boy or girl when we meet in heaven? How can I ever explain or justify what I've done?*

Elaine had confessed her mistake to God. She'd understood the Bible teaching that the Lord forgives and forgets. But she had been unwilling to forgive herself. She'd made reliving her greatest regret part of her daily routine.[3]

This isn't how God wants us to live! As Randy Alcorn has written,

> Refusing to forgive ourselves is an act of pride—it's making ourselves and our sins bigger than God and His grace.[4]

The Lord's power is absolute, and His Word is the last word. When He grants forgiveness, it's *done*. We can't see the way forward if we're always looking in the rearview mirror of our past errors.

The feeling of being unable to forgive yourself may be a sign of a lack of trust in God. You will need to spend more time with Him. As you develop that relationship, you'll begin to see that He really does have the power to pardon any sin, including yours.

You may be struggling also with the actual process of letting go. Try this: On a piece of paper, write down everything about the incident causing your guilt. Spare no details. Then, make a conscious decision to put it behind you forever. Light the paper with a match and watch it burn—make sure every inch turns to ash. This ritual of literally destroying a piece of your past can be a powerful reminder that it's no longer part of your life.

AM I WILLING TO FOCUS ON THE TRUTH?

It isn't easy to let go of guilt if your spouse, child, friend, or colleague continues to point out your past missteps. When your daughter says, "I may love you, but I'll never forgive you for driving Dad away," the pain can feel almost like a pounding jackhammer. In a similar way, after the death of a spouse, an empty home can be an agonizing daily reminder of all the times you spoke harshly and now wish you hadn't.

If you've followed the steps suggested above, it's time to focus on the truth, regardless of what others say or what circumstances show. *You are forgiven.* There is nothing more for you to complete, no more duties to perform, no one else you must confess to. God's Word is final. *Allow your heart and mind to be at peace.*

If you're struggling with this pattern of continually reliving your failures, I encourage you to decide now to break the cycle. You have the power to choose your thoughts!

Begin by writing down or typing out a long list of positive "thought balloons" that you can grab whenever your mind starts to move in a negative direction. It might be a series of blessings in your life (e.g., family and friends). It might be examples of how God has been faithful to you over the years. It might be the simplest pleasures you enjoy. At the end of each thought balloon, write "I am forgiven."

Consider yourself an athlete in training—you must teach your mind to reach for a balloon every time you're tempted to revive your guilt over a past mistake. Remember: *Once you give it to God, it's gone.*

Growing Stronger

No one enjoys screwing up and traveling through the garden of guilt. It can be among the most devastating journeys we ever take. What comes out of the experience, however, often makes us stronger and better people. For instance:

- We gain a clearer picture of our weaknesses and of areas where we need help.
- We understand that *all* people are flawed and need forgiveness.
- We use our regrets to chart a new direction for ourselves.
- We learn to be more open with others about our vulnerabilities.

- We develop deeper relationships.
- We grow a stronger faith.
- We discover that forgiving ourselves is a healthy process we can incorporate into our lives.

Forgiving yourself is a huge step toward freedom and peace. Review the suggestions provided in this chapter and know that it *will* happen. Letting go of your guilt is one act you'll never regret.

CHAPTER 10

WORRY LESS, LAUGH MORE

What soap is to the body, laughter is to the soul.

YIDDISH PROVERB

Bonnie Kopp's diagnosis of breast cancer was no laughing matter. The months that followed the news were difficult—filled with doctor appointments, medical research, radiation treatments, the worry and anxiety that accompany any life-threatening condition.

Bonnie wasn't used to facing so serious a crisis day after day. She'd grown up with a wonderful ability to see the joy in life, and if she didn't see it, she found ways to create it. For instance, she and her twin sister, Connie, used to double date. Sometimes the sisters excused themselves to go to the restroom, swapped clothes there, and then returned to see how long it took their dates to figure out the switch!

Bonnie found the weeks of visits to the cold, sterile radiation lab depressing. The members of the hospital staff were so desensitized to their dying patients that they rarely made eye contact. It was gloomy to the point that Bonnie decided something had to be done. When Connie called to say she was passing through town, Bonnie had an inspiration.

Soon after, Bonnie and Connie arrived at the lab for Bonnie's appointment. The nurses were too busy to notice that two women had entered the changing room. Moments later, Connie—wearing Bonnie's gown—emerged.

"Good morning," the nurse said. "How are you today?"

"Oh, it's been such a busy morning," Connie said. "I'm feeling a little confused." She hopped onto the table for patients.

"My goodness, you *are* confused!" the nurse said. "Your head is at the wrong end of the table."

Connie was nervous and had trouble unbuttoning her gown. "I just don't know what's wrong with me," she said. "I'm obviously not myself today."

Early in Bonnie's treatment, the nurses had tattooed small, permanent dots onto her chest where the radiation was to be administered. Now, examining Connie, the nurse couldn't find them. "There are no tattoos!" she exclaimed. Another nurse came running and also was baffled. "I've never seen anything like this before," she said.

Bonnie finally opened the dressing room door and said, in a stern voice, "What are you doing, giving radiation to the wrong patient?"

A technician nearly fainted, a nurse screamed, and the rest of the staff burst into laughter.

Later, Connie explained the ruckus to a man and his wife in the waiting room. The wife doubled over with laughter. The husband hugged her and said, "Thank you. Thank you for doing this. My wife thinks she is dying, and this is the first time I've seen her laugh in three months."

Meanwhile, the doctor administering Bonnie's treatment told her, "You brought more healing today than any radiation ever could. Thank you for being brave enough to pull the switch—and for giving everyone a good, hard laugh!"[1]

We live in an age that's increasingly fast-paced and uncertain. When a crisis is added to our plate, it's natural for our worry and anxiety levels to shoot off the charts.

Unfortunately, this makes it twice as difficult for us to respond well to the new challenge. Anxiety can cause heart palpitations, shortness of breath, nausea, the shakes, tense muscles, clenched teeth, loss of appetite, lack of sleep, anger, loneliness, depression, and plenty more symptoms we'd just as soon avoid.

Worry, meanwhile, is like negative meditation. Worry is a continual rehashing of potential disastrous outcomes. Worry robs us of energy that could be focused on the actual problem. As the old saying goes, "Worry is like a rocking chair. It gives you something to do but never gets you anywhere."

That's why, especially when we're up against a potentially devastating life-turn, we need to counteract our tendency to worry and feel anxious. One of the best lines of defense is a sense of humor. Let's talk about ways to worry less and laugh more.

"Worry Busters"

Jesus made it plain where He stood on the subject of worry:

Do not worry about your life, what you will eat or drink; or about your body, what you will wear. . . . Who of you by worrying can add a single hour to his life? (Matthew 6:25, 27).

Yet we still struggle with fears about the future. Worry can be a hard habit to break.

The next time you find yourself dwelling on your concerns, try a few of the following ideas for a more restful state of mind.

WORRY BUSTER #1: TRY TO CALM DOWN.

If you're starting down the worry path, change directions by taking a pair of long, deep breaths. Ask your spouse (or a professional) to massage your neck, shoulders, and hand muscles. Take a brief walk; movement will help you release the tension. Replace your negative thinking by meditating on a peaceful image, idea, or verse of Scripture. One of my favorite things to do is put on worship music. I find it hard to worry about me when I'm thinking about Him.

WORRY BUSTER #2: SORT OUT YOUR CONCERNS.

Again, Reinhold Niebuhr's "Serenity Prayer," adopted by Alcoholics Anonymous, begins with the words, "God, grant me the serenity to accept the things I cannot change; courage to change the things I can; and wisdom to know the difference."

If you're weary from worry, try writing out your concerns and then talking them over with a confidante. Separate what you can influence from what you have no control over. Resolve to let go of the things you aren't able to fix. If you can't do anything about it, why worry?

WORRY BUSTER #3: TAKE ACTION IF YOU CAN.

Sometimes our anxiety stems from avoiding the issue. If you've been injured in a serious accident and are worried you'll never regain your health, you may be afraid to find out. Your fears can become self-fulfilling.

Instead of fearing the worst, decide to position yourself for success. Talk to doctors and patients who've suffered similar injuries. Read up on the latest medical information. Develop a plan that incorporates what's worked for others but takes into account your specific desires and needs. You can eliminate most of your worries with positive action.

WORRY BUSTER #4: TURN OVER YOUR WORRIES
TO THE LORD.

Ultimately, trusting God is the *only* effective response to our tendency to worry. When you do, according to the apostle Paul, "you will experience God's peace, which is far more wonderful than the human mind can understand" (Philippians 4:7 NLT). If you're drowning in worry, set aside extra time, daily, to pray and meditate on the Word of God.

WORRY BUSTER #5: WHEN WORRIES RETURN, DISTRACT YOURSELF.

For many, bedtime is the moment when worries weigh us down the most. No matter when your worry time seems to fall, find a way to short-circuit the pattern.

If worries begin to get you down at night, you may want to read a book, fold some clothes, or take a short walk around the house. If it's during the day, maybe you can write an encouraging note to a friend or take the dog out. Cut off worries immediately with a positive distraction that will focus your thinking in a new and better direction.

WORRY BUSTER #6: BUILD YOUR TRUST MUSCLES.

Trust is an acquired habit. If you're facing a crisis, much of your worry may be based on trying to handle everything on your own. You must give the people who care about you a chance to help. Make an effort to trust them beyond what feels comfortable.

Maybe you hate to trouble them with asking for help preparing a meal—try it anyway. You'll probably discover that they're happy to pitch in. While you're at it, push yourself to trust the Lord beyond what feels comfortable as well. You'll find that the more you put in His hands, the greater your peace.[2]

Worry and anxiety are like heavy weights that trail along behind you wherever you go. The more you worry, the heavier they feel. Worrying never adds to your ability to cope—it only slows you down.

It's time to *release* your worry weights. Drop them in an alley somewhere. Better yet, hand them over to God and trust Him to deal with your problems. He can see the future you can't and knows exactly what to do.

Good Medicine

If you've ever heard me speak, you know I like to have fun. I don't have a speech in my files that doesn't have some sort of goofy story or joke in it.

As a guest speaker, I don't know the people at each event or what they're going through, so I try to build a bridge through humor. I usually use it at the beginning of a talk to get the audience's attention. A smile is a universal language; it breaks down walls, it can start relationships, and it can open the heart and mind to listen and learn.

It's been said that the average child laughs several hundred times per day, while the typical adult laughs only a few times in those same twenty-four hours. It seems most of us lose our ability to laugh at our circumstances as we age. We *need* to laugh, however. It's good medicine for our bodies, minds, and spirits. If we can recapture childlike glee, we'll bounce back more quickly from life's inevitable hardships and leave our worries behind.

Norman Cousins, in *Anatomy of an Illness as Perceived by the Patient*, wrote of how he fought a crippling form of arthritis by reading and watching humorous books and movies during the day. A favorite was Marx Brothers films: "I made the joyous discovery that ten minutes of genuine belly laughter had an anesthetic effect and would give me at least two hours of pain-free sleep," he said. "When the pain-killing effect of the laughter wore off, we would switch on the motion-picture projector again, and, not infrequently, it would lead to another pain-free sleep interval."[3] His disease went into remission, and he lived years longer than anticipated by his doctors.

Studies since have shown that laughter does indeed prompt a host of positive influences. It stimulates the release of endorphins and serotonin, hormones that create feelings of euphoria, love, and happiness, and it suppresses stress hormones. It also produces a psychological phenomenon known as "facial feedback," where adopting a specific expression can lead you to experience the corresponding emotion. In other words, if you put on a happy face, you *may* begin to feel happy!

Laughter likewise reduces tension and stress, strengthens the immune system, and protects the heart by improving the function of blood vessels, encouraging blood flow and improving cholesterol levels and blood pressure.

Finally, a little levity is good for your social life. Most people are attracted to positive, jolly personalities. The old saying, "When you laugh, the world laughs with you" is founded in truth.

Guffaws don't come so easily when we're grieving or in the midst of difficulty. All the same, the hard times are when we need humor most. Kevin Jones was one man who kept his sense of humor during the most arduous challenge of his life. While dealing with increasing paralysis from Lou Gehrig's disease (ALS), he was asked to describe the worst thing about his condition. "My wife's driving!" he said. "She has to take me everywhere."[4]

Comedian Milton Berle once said that "laughter is an instant vacation." Here are some suggestions to remind you that even in grim circumstances, your laugh vacation is only a moment away.

Keep (and keep building) a stockpile of tummy ticklers.

Start collecting favorite movies, comic strips, jokes, greeting cards, videos, and stories that you can turn to for encouragement when everything around you seems a disaster. Here's a handful of misprints and misstatements from church bulletins to get you started:

- "Ushers will eat latecomers."
- "The third verse of 'Blessed Assurance' will be sung without musical accomplishment."
- "Tonight's sermon: 'What Is Hell?' Come early and listen to our choir practice."

- "Barbara remains in the hospital. She is having trouble sleeping and requests tapes of Pastor Jack's sermons."
- "The choir will meet at the Larsen house for fun and sinning."
- "The sermon this morning: 'Jesus Walks on Water.' The sermon tonight: 'Searching for Jesus.' "
- "The cost for attending the Fasting Prayer conference includes meals."
- "Ladies, don't forget the rummage sale. It is a good chance to get rid of things not worth keeping around the house. Bring your husbands!"[5]

LAUGH AT YOURSELF.

Life's problems don't seem quite so serious if we're able to poke fun at our mishaps. Think of incidents where what you said and did turned into what's now a funny or embarrassing story. Find someone who doesn't know the tale and, without putting yourself down, share the story and a good laugh.

GET SILLY.

Carve out time to play games that force you to be silly. Invite people over who you know are goofy and will have a blast playing. It doesn't take long with the right group gathered together to see the craziness begin. Don't wait until you're in the mood—schedule weekly or even daily playtime!

SEEK COMIC RELIEF.

Many clubs and restaurants host comedians and improvisational comedy groups, and many local performers appear for free or at minimal cost. Schedule a night to take in an act with a spouse or friend. If none are available in your area, check the TV, or rent a comedy DVD (a little research will turn up "clean" comedians) and laugh the night away.

BE A KID AGAIN.

What are some of the things that made you smile and laugh when you were a kid? Thrill rides? Pillow fights? Go-Karts? Roller skating? Playing in the rain?

Now's the perfect time to get in touch with your inner child. Find a friend, get in the car, go to the amusement park or the beach, do whatever you need to set the mood, and turn back the clock. It's never too late to rediscover your childhood.

Rabbi Moshe Waldoks once wrote, "A sense of humor can help you overlook the unattractive, tolerate the unpleasant, cope with the unexpected, and smile through the unbearable." Humor brings perspective, balance, and healing back to hurting souls. It is a way of shining joy into the darkest corners. It's also a great way to banish worries and anxiety from your mind.

Don't ever forget: He who laughs, lasts.

CHAPTER 11

HOLDING OUT FOR HOPE

Where there's life, there's hope.

TERENCE

My friends Roger and Becca Davis well remember the day they received the awful news. Their son Sterling, not quite five, had been vomiting for no apparent reason. At one point, when Sterling threw up in the car, Becca just knew that whatever was wrong was serious. She began to cry.

A battery of tests led to a meeting with a radiologist. "There really is no other way to tell you this," he said. "Your son has a mass in his head."

For Becca, the fact that the enemy could be malignant was especially frightening. She'd lost her mother to cancer after a long battle. The possible realization that her family was fighting it again left her feeling paralyzed when facing difficult decisions about Sterling's treatment.

Roger, meanwhile, was haunted by questions. *Will Sterling live?* he wondered. *Will he make it to high school? Will he be able to play sports?*

As Sterling endured one surgery after another, the Davis family fought to maintain a sense of normalcy for their other children—and to keep up their sense of hope.

While you may not have faced *this* crisis, I'll bet you can relate to the feeling of sailing along smoothly and suddenly finding yourself in the waves, dog-paddling in desperation. It happens to all of us.

You walk into your teen's bedroom looking for clothes to wash and find drugs. You visit the clinic for what's supposed to be a routine appointment and leave with a life-altering diagnosis. You answer the phone and hear the dreaded words, "There's been a terrible accident." Your spouse walks out the front door uttering the unthinkable: "I just can't be with you anymore."

Your knockdown may not come from a single, devastating upper-cut. Maybe instead it's the result of a series of jabs that wears you down, leading from tiredness and soreness to fatigue and frustration and, finally, to exhaustion and anguish. After days, weeks, months . . . years of emotional turmoil, of caring for loved ones, of being the strong one that everybody comes to depend on, sometimes you just *wear out*. You hit the mat because you no longer have the strength, or the balance, to stand.

Whatever the cause, something can happen to us when we suffer injuries like these. They can erode our belief in a brighter future. Just getting up in the morning can become a chore.

We lose energy. We lose optimism. We lose motivation. We lose faith in ourselves, in others, and in God.

We lose *hope*.

Has your hope been stripped away? Are you sleepwalking through each day because you no longer believe in or have interest in tomorrow?

It doesn't have to be this way. In truth, your hopelessness can be a catalyst for steering your life toward something wonderful.

To get on that course, though, we have some work to do. Let's start by taking this simple quick-hope quiz. Choose the answer that best describes your feelings, or how you likely would feel.

***Envision:* You're struggling in the class that's supposed to teach you how to sing, cook, or write.**

1. ___ I know it's a matter of time until I get the hang of it.
2. ___ I'm having doubts that I'll catch on.
3. ___ I'll know I've made a terrible mistake and that I'll never get it.

Envision: You've been laid off from a job you truly enjoyed.

1. ___ I believe something better must be around the corner.
2. ___ I wonder if I'll find another job that's comparable.
3. ___ I'm sure I'll never find enjoyable work again.

Envision: A friend asks you to list your goals and dreams.

1. ___ I can identify several with enthusiasm.
2. ___ I have a few but aren't sure how many are possible.
3. ___ I say to my friend, "What's the point?"

Envision: You're contemplating the future.

1. ___ I figure the best is yet to come.
2. ___ I'm optimistic yet realistic about what's ahead.
3. ___ I expect life to get even worse.

Envision: You're pondering the state of your relationships with family and friends.

1. ___ I feel connected and expect to grow even closer to them in the future.
2. ___ I value my family and friends but would like to be closer.
3. ___ I feel lonely and figure it will always be this way.

Envision: You're taking stock of your life.

1. ___ I feel blessed.
2. ___ I've had my ups and downs but am hanging in there.
3. ___ I wonder what went wrong.

Add up your "points" based on the number for each answer you chose. (Each #1 response is one point; #2, two; #3, three.)

If you're in the six-to-eight range, you are an off-the-charts optimist—you should be writing this chapter.

If your total is between nine and fourteen, you're often hopeful but balance that perspective with a healthy dose of realism.

If you scored fifteen points or higher, you're probably suffering from hope deficiency. Keep reading. You need to take action—right now.

From Hurting to Healing

Hopelessness is nothing to mess around with. This place is okay to visit, but you definitely don't want to stay. As someone once said, "Without hope, life is meaningless. Without hope, life is meaning less and less." If you don't have hope, you are hurting.

When you feel there's nothing to look forward to, you need a kick-start to get your engine running again. A few simple steps can at least get you moving forward again. I strongly encourage you to look over the following list and commit to completing at least one of these tasks every day for a week. In fact, I highly recommend more than one.

Make a conscious effort to identify what you're lacking the most, and start there. If your hope tank is empty, this isn't an optional exercise or something to fit in if you have time. I challenge you to finish this assignment. You won't regret it.

- *Do something that will improve your body.* Maybe you don't exercise much (or at all) and would benefit from a walk. Perhaps you've been short on sleep and need an afternoon off (or three!) to nap. Maybe it's been years since you rode a bike or took a swim. Go for it and see how it feels.
- *Do something to lift your spirits.* What makes you feel good? A cup of tea and a good book? A luxurious bath? Manicure, pedicure,

or massage? Shopping with the gals? . . . A movie? Round of golf? Hiking or climbing? Pizza with the guys? What's that one thing you've been itching to try and haven't given yourself permission to do? Assuming it doesn't break your budget and add stress to your life, now is the time.

- *Change your environment.* Sometimes a few spatial adjustments can alter your outlook in a big way. Rearrange the furniture in your living room. Paint the bedroom. Open the blinds. Spend an afternoon at the lake or library. Do something different to your surroundings to give yourself a fresh perspective.

- *Count your blessings.* It sounds old school, but making a list of everything you're thankful for really can inject a dose of hope into your heart. Don't knock it until you've come up with at least ten items for your list.

- *Open up to a trusted friend.* So often, we keep our heavier thoughts to ourselves. Most true friends, however, are more sympathetic than we think—and they've probably harbored a few dark ideas themselves. The act of talking over your emotions and hearing a confidante's take on the matter can illuminate problems in ways you've never imagined.

- *Give yourself quiet time.* The hustle and bustle of daily life is enough to weigh down anyone and cause hope loss. Thirty minutes of peaceful retreat, whether it's first thing in the morning, during a lunch break, or any other time, can be a great way to renew yourself. Turn off all noisemakers (TV, computer, phone et al.) and let your mind settle. If you're a person of faith, this is a perfect time to pray and reconnect with God.

Now I have another suggestion. I want you to stop reading and put this book down. Take some time to fully explore the recommendations (above) that call to your heart. Pay attention to your answers. You're already on your way to healing and renewed hope.

Prognosis for Hope

Good to have you back! How was it? I hope some of these steps produced at least a hint of a smile on your lips and a tinge of hope in your heart.

Please don't be discouraged if the feeling was fleeting. This is only the beginning. The steps were designed to rekindle a sense of forward movement and optimism. They also were a way to take your life temperature and discover a diagnosis for your condition.

Think back on the previous week. What actions gave you the most satisfaction or even excitement? Which created a flash of anticipation? Which would you most like to continue with this week? Most likely, your responses will center around one of three dimensions lacking in your life and draining your hope (though it's possible that all three need attention): physical, emotional, and/or spiritual.

PHYSICAL: SLOW DOWN THE ROLLER COASTER.

Let's talk first about the physical aspect. The single dad who's juggling two part-time jobs with raising his kids, the woman who's putting in too many late-night hours to finish that big work project, and the parents of a newborn who're wishing for just one good night of sleep know all about what it means to feel run down. We're persistently burdened with responsibilities and bombarded constantly by the demands of others. We live in a fast-food, fast-lane culture that expects results *now*.

Here's the deal, though—society is not in charge of your life. *You* are. While in certain given moments there will be things you simply must do, in the bigger picture, when your friends, your parents, your employers, or the TV networks demand (overtly or implicitly) that you stick to their schedule, you don't have to. In fact, the people closest to you will appreciate it (later, if not sooner) when you start taking care of yourself. You'll discover that you're more rested, more joyful, and better able to relate with others when you're not plodding from one event to the next like a zombie.

Easier said than done? You bet. But you truly *can* live with the disappointment in your mother's voice. It actually *is* an option to negotiate with your boss (in a professional manner) about extending the deadline for that supposedly vital project. You really *are* able to learn to say no the next time someone asks you to do, well, just about anything.

Rest, recreation, good fuel (food), and exercise are what keep your body going. Start small, but devote attention to each, starting today. Jot down one, two, or three basic steps you can implement over the next week in each area. It might be making bedtime a priority every other night, dirty dishes or not. It could be committing to taking a walk three mornings a week. Maybe it's bringing healthy lunches to work.

You aren't indestructible. If you don't take care of you, ultimately— now, soon, or eventually—there won't be any *you* left to take care of everyone and everything else.

Whether it's a hamster wheel, a treadmill, or a roller coaster you've been stuck on, it's been robbing you of hope, and now's the time to put on the brakes.

EMOTIONAL: CHANNEL YOUR FEELINGS.

Regarding your emotional state, if you're feeling hopeless, your feelings may be fluctuating like a yo-yo. Life's consistent stresses— family disagreements, conflicts with friends, paying bills, managing rebellious kids, dealing with an ornery manager—are enough to upset anyone. Throw in a surprise roundhouse punch, though, and emotions themselves quickly can seem overwhelming.

You're not a robot. It's inevitable that you're going to respond to frustrating or crushing circumstances with debilitating feelings. That's okay. What's important to remember is that you don't have to be ruled by them. You can choose how to direct those strong emotions.

I'm not saying you should ignore or "stuff" your feelings; that's just as harmful as letting emotions run your life. I am suggesting that you channel your responses in healthy ways. For instance, keep a record of your feelings about what you're going through. Talk them out with your spouse or a friend. Give yourself permission to cry. Pray. Look for any trace of humor you can find in the situation.

———————

With all this said, there may be seasons when nothing you do sparks even an ember of hope. If some or all of the following sound like your situation even after applying the advice in this book, it might be time to speak to a professional counselor or pastor.

- You're consistently afraid that something awful is going to happen to you or someone you love.
- You're so emotionally numb that you can't think straight or accomplish simple tasks.
- You're gaining or losing weight for no apparent reason.
- Repeatedly you've been unable to sleep at night.
- Your family and friends are concerned about your behavior and well-being.
- You have recurring thoughts about taking your life.

Perhaps the best way to place your crisis—and your response—in perspective is to look at it from God's viewpoint. Maybe you can see what I mean from this conversation:

A man in the midst of a financial collapse went to a pastor to seek counsel.
>*"I've lost everything," he lamented.*
>*"I'm sorry to hear you've lost your faith."*
>*"No," the man protested. "I haven't lost my faith."*
>*"Then I'm sad to hear you've lost your character."*
>*"I didn't say that," he objected. "I still have my character."*
>*"Well, certainly I'm sorry to hear you've lost your salvation."*
>*"That isn't what I said," the man went on. "I have not lost my salvation."*

"You have your faith, your character, and your salvation," mused the pastor. "Seems to me, you've lost nothing that actually matters."[1]

SPIRITUAL: RENEW YOUR FAITH.

Last, while I don't know where you stand in terms of faith and belief in God, I do know, from experience and from observations of people around the world, that we all seem to have a deep-seated sense of the spiritual, as well as a need to discover what this means. My own journey has led me to an unshakable trust that Jesus Christ is the Son of God and that He loves me. I've committed my life to Him.

I believe that Jesus loves you too.

Another thing I've observed: It's when people are at a place of genuine despair and desperation that they are most ready to hear God's voice. It appears that the Lord sometimes allows us to experience crisis and hope loss in order to get our attention and draw us closer to Him.

Remember Roger and Becca Davis? Their circumstances are so overwhelming that they feel they have no other option but to rely on the Lord. "It hasn't been hard to trust God," Roger reflects. "How can you not, when you have nothing else? You can't manage the situation. You can't heal Sterling. But God can."

Although Sterling's brain tumor is not cancerous, it's in a very difficult area to reach, and he continues to have frequent seizures. Roger and Becca don't know how things will turn out, but they are finding their family's faith strengthened because of the experience.

"When Sterling shows signs of joy and hope, when he says to the nurse, 'It's okay because God is with me,' it makes us feel like parents cheering for their son after he scores the winning touchdown," Roger says. "We understand that sometimes God gets glory from delivering us from trials and sometimes He gets glory from how we walk through our trials. We're just trusting a God who loves our son even more than we do."

I don't mean to over-spiritualize your troubles. But I do want to point out the possibility that if you're down and out of hope, you may be exactly where God wants you. This may be a significant turning point in your life, a time to investigate, discover, renew, or deepen your faith. Ask yourself these foundational questions:

- Could my hopelessness have anything to do with my distance from God?
- Might God be trying to tell me something here?
- What new opportunities may be opening up for me at this time?
- When has a time of despair led to positive changes in my life and in the lives of others?
- Am I looking and listening for guidance toward that next hopeful step?

Though it's hard to remember when hope seems lost, God has our lives under control and can be trusted to know what's best for us:

> Those who know your name will trust in you,
> for you, Lord, have never forsaken those who seek you.
> (Psalm 9:10)

Even better, He is our source.

> May your unfailing love rest upon us, O Lord,
> even as we put our hope in you. (Psalm 33:22)

Talk to Him. Listen, and watch, for His wisdom. Wait patiently for that moment when you can get up off the mat, see the reasons behind your challenges, and cheerfully renew your hope. I promise you: It *will* be worth the wait.

STILL STANDING

A bend in the road is not the end of the road . . . unless you fail to make the turn.

ANONYMOUS

When the unimaginable happens, it's after the shock begins to wear off that the doubts creep in.

You lose your job and lie in bed, thinking, *How am I going to pay for our next meal, let alone next month's rent?*

You suffer a heart attack and wonder, *Will I ever be able to live like a normal person again?*

Your spouse succumbs to illness and you cry out, *"How can I even make it through life without my soul mate?"*

This book has been an attempt to begin responding to those kinds of questions. I hope you've realized that even in the worst of circumstances there is strength that can carry us through: strength in faith, strength in love, strength in courage, strength in determination, strength in resilience, strength in hope. These, combined with proven strategies for coping with crisis, can enable you not only to survive your knockdown but also get back up a stronger and wiser person.[1]

> Be strong and courageous. . . . Do not be terrified; do not be discouraged, for the Lord your God will be with you wherever you go. (Joshua 1:6, 9)

Though it may be hard to imagine if you're experiencing major pain right now, you can know there *is* an amazing life full of hope and joy waiting for you. Remember that God created you and loves you. I'll bet there are people in your life who cherish you too.

If you've been knocked off your feet: Pray. Trust in God. Take care of yourself. Allow family and friends to love you. You may be down . . . but the time is coming when you'll be ready to get back up.

NOTES

Chapter 1: Back in the Game

1. Kay Campbell, "Life in the Recession" in *The Huntsville Times,* January 15, 2010. *http://blog.al.com/breaking/2010/01/life_in_the_recession_despite.html.*

2. Jim Martin, "Men Bear the Brunt of Recession in Erie County" in *Erie Times-News,* April 18, 2010. *www.goerie.com/apps/pbcs.dll/article?AID=/20100418/BUSINESS 0201/304139920/0/business.*

Chapter 2: The Power of Perseverance

1. Stormie Omartian, *The Power of a Praying Wife* (Eugene, OR: Harvest House, 1997), 16–17; and Stormie Omartian, *The Power of a Praying Husband* (Eugene, OR: Harvest House, 2001), 18, 21–22.

2. Cal Ripken Jr., *Get in the Game* (New York: Gotham, 2007), 60.

3. Omartian, *Praying Wife,* 16-17 and *Praying Husband,* 18, 21-22.

Chapter 3: The Hurt That Heals

1. Philip Yancey, *Where Is God When It Hurts?* (Grand Rapids, MI: Zondervan, 1977, 1990), 27–28.

2. Marlo Schalesky, *Empty Womb, Aching Heart* (Minneapolis: Bethany House, 2001), 113–116.

3. Mary Frances Bowley, *A League of Dangerous Women* (Colorado Springs: Multnomah, 2006), 23–24.

4. Dr. Mark R. Laaser, *Healing the Wounds of Sexual Addiction* (Grand Rapids, MI: Zondervan, 1992, 1996, 2004), 135.

5. Bowley, 22, 34.

6. Schalesky, 116.

Chapter 4: From Denial to Renewal

1. Pam Vredevelt, *Angel Behind the Rocking Chair* (Sisters, OR: Multnomah, 1997), 15–19.

Chapter 5: Turning Anger Into Positive Action

1. See John Ortberg, "Anger" at *http://www.buildingchurchleaders.com/devotions/2004/aug2004.html*, August 1, 2004.
2. "Boiling Point Report 2008," *http://www.angermanage.co.uk/data.html*.
3. Elizabeth B. Brown, *Living Successfully with Screwed-Up People* (Grand Rapids, MI: Revell, 1999), 128–132.
4. Adapted from Brown, ibid., 132.

Chapter 6: The Best Deal You'll Ever Make

1. Elisabeth Kübler-Ross, *On Death and Dying* (New York: Scribner, 1969), 95.
2. Joyce Landorf, *Mourning Song* (Old Tappan, NJ: Fleming H. Revell, 1974), 83–84.
3. Ibid., 84.
4. Sue Augustine, *Sanity Secrets for Stressed-Out Women* (Eugene, OR: Harvest House, 2009), 70–71.

Chapter 7: A Measure of Responsibility

1. From Paul Prather, "Blaming Others Leads Nowhere," September 11, 2010, *www.kentucky.com/2010/09/11/1429797/paul-prather-blaming-others-leads.html*.
2. Kathy Peel, *Desperate Households* (Carol Stream, IL: Tyndale, 2007), 209.

Chapter 8: Finding Freedom in Forgiveness

1. Tom Bowers, "Someone I Had to Forgive" in *Guideposts*, January 1999, quoted in Lourdes Morales-Gudmundsson, *I Forgive You, But* . . . (Nampa, ID: Pacific, 2007), 136–137.
2. David F. Allen, *Shattering the Gods Within* (McLean, VA: Curtain Call, 2004), 161.
3. Corrie ten Boom, *The Hiding Place* (Chappaqua, NY: Chosen), from quotations in Dr. James and Shirley Dobson, *Night Light* (Sisters, OR: Multnomah, 2000), 184–186.
4. Neil T. Anderson and Charles Mylander, *The Christ-Centered Marriage* (Ventura, CA: Gospel Light/Regal, 1996), quoted in ibid., 187.
5. Ken Sande, *The Peacemaker* (Grand Rapids, MI: Baker, 1997), 189–190.
6. "Forgiveness Steps" adapted from Dr. Steve Stephens and Alice Gray, *The Worn Out Woman* (Sisters, OR: Multnomah, 2004), see 158–163.
7. Bowers, 136–137.

Chapter 9: Letting Go of Guilt

1. Rick Warren, *The Purpose Driven Life* (Grand Rapids, MI: Zondervan, 2002), 27–28.
2. Dr. James and Shirley Dobson, *Night Light for Parents* (Sisters, OR: Multnomah, 2002), 224.
3. Dennis Kizziar, *Hope for the Troubled Heart* (Bend, OR: Maverick, 2008), 35–36.
4. Randy Alcorn, *The Grace and Truth Paradox* (Sisters, OR: Multnomah, 2003), 84.

Chapter 10: Worry Less, Laugh More

1. Pam Vredevelt, *Espresso for a Woman's Spirit, Book 2* (Sisters, OR: Multnomah, 2001), 23–27.

2. "Worry Busters" adapted from Dr. Steve Stephens and Alice Gray, *The Worn Out Woman*, see 170–175.

3. Norman Cousins, *Anatomy of an Illness as Perceived by the Patient* (New York: W.W. Norton & Co., 2001), 43.

4. Dr. James and Shirley Dobson, *Night Light* (Sisters, OR: Multnomah, 2000), 258.

5. Ibid., 260.

Chapter 11: Holding Out for Hope

1. Adapted from citation in Max Lucado, *Traveling Light: Releasing the Burdens You Were Never Intended to Bear* (Nashville: Thomas Nelson, 2006), 33.

Epilogue: Still Standing

1. If you're interested in reading more about people who've been battered by life's storms but have emerged still standing and have learned how to thrive again—people who've overcome terrific setbacks *and* their own significant doubts—here are just a few suggestions for starting out. These are the stories of ordinary people, just like you and me, who've confronted physical hardship, brutal betrayal, devastating mistakes, the loss of loved ones . . . and they're facing their futures with confidence. Charlie and Lucy Wedemeyer, *Charlie's Victory* (Grand Rapids, MI: Zondervan, 1993) [also see *www.wedemeyer.org*]; Mary Frances Bowley, *A League of Dangerous Women* (Colorado Springs: Multnomah, 2006); Jim Daly, *Stronger* (Colorado Springs: David C. Cook, 2010); Lisa Ryan, *Generation Esther* (Sisters, OR: Multnomah, 2003).

About the Author

Jeremy Kingsley is the founder of OneLife Ministries. Having been through his own hard times, he now travels nationally with messages of hope and encouragement. The author of four books, Jeremy is also a consultant for churches, parachurch organizations, and corporations, and teaches leadership development. He and his wife, Dawn, live in Columbia, South Carolina, with their two sons, Jaden and Dylan.

OneLife
M I N I S T R I E S

Teaching People, Loving Individuals

Would you like to have Jeremy Kingsley, author of
Getting Back Up When Life Knocks You Down
speak at your church or special event?

Contact:
OneLife Ministries
1-803-315-2788

Learn more about OneLife Ministries and Jeremy Kingsley at
www.jeremykingsley.com